Words for the Journey for Kids

Ten-Minute Prayer Services for Schools

Lisa Freemantle and Les Miller

NOVALIS

© 2010 Novalis Publishing Inc.

Cover: Blaine Herrmann
Cover artwork: Lynne McIlvride Evans (www.mcilvride-evans.com)
Layout: Audrey Wells

Published by Novalis
10 Lower Spadina Avenue, Suite 400
Toronto, Ontario, Canada
M5V 2Z2

www.novalis.ca

Library and Archives Canada Cataloguing in Publication

Freemantle, Lisa, 1962-
    Words for the journey : ten-minute prayer services
for schools / Lisa Freemantle, Leslie Miller.

Includes bibliographical references and index.
ISBN 978-2-89646-239-1

    1. Schools--Prayers. 2. Catholic Church--Liturgy--Texts.
3. Catholic Church--Prayers and devotions. I. Miller,
Leslie, 1952- II. Title.

BV283.S3F74 2010   242'.82   C2010-903519-4
Printed in Canada.

We acknowledge the financial support of the Government of Canada through the Book Publishing Industry
Development Program (BPIDP) for our publishing activities.

5 4 3 2 1   14 13 12 11 10

Acknowledgements

We wish to thank those who helped in the creation of this book,
both materially and spiritually,
especially our beloved spouses and children;

our colleagues in the York Catholic District School Board
and the Ontario educational community;
as well as Joe Sinasac, Grace Deutsch, and
Anne Louise Mahoney at Novalis.
May their journeys always be blessed with words of wisdom.

Contents

Introduction

Our teaching vocation as Catholic educators is a commitment to share our faith with our students. Praying with them is a key part of their moral, spiritual and academic development and is the most important activity we do with them.

Words for the Journey for Kids is a collection of 50 original, ready-to-use prayer services that cover liturgical as well as secular themes. These are organized by month and can be used either in the classroom or with the whole school. Some of these prayer services have parts for students. Others are more contemplative. All are intended to involve many students, yet can easily be adapted to suit users' needs. Although some prayer services follow the general pattern of the Liturgy of the Word, some deviate from this form because of the nature of the prayer.

Words for the Journey for Kids is designed to be engaging yet meaningful for students and user-friendly for teachers. For each prayer service, we offer ideas for setting up the prayer space. You may want to add school or class symbols to these suggestions. To reinforce the message that all themes are rooted in the word of God, each prayer service contains a reading from the Bible.

Here are some other things to keep in mind when you are preparing a prayer service:

- Read the suggestions for each prayer service that are found in the Appendix.

- Choose readers ahead of time.

- Explain logistics for rituals (such as where or when to stand, or other actions) before you begin the prayer.

- Make the sign of the cross together at the beginning and at the end of each service (where you see a "+" in the text).

- Include the doxology (*For the kingdom, the power, and the glory are yours, now and for ever. Amen.*) at the end of the Lord's Prayer.

- Add live or recorded music to these prayer services if you wish.

- Where appropriate (particularly after a scripture reading), incorporate a few moments of silence into the prayers.

It is important to share our Catholic tradition with our students. Praying with *Words for the Journey for Kids* is one way to help them grow in faith and love.

Lisa Freemantle and Les Miller

September

1. The Journey Begins

May the Lord bless you
and take care of you.

(Numbers 6:24)

Opening Prayer

+ Loving God,
you are kindness and caring,
you are wondrous and wise,
you are our friend and guide,
you are our deepest truth.

You bring us together
to learn,
to play,
to worship together.
Be with us and guide us
now and throughout the school year.

Jesus Blesses the Children
(adapted from Matthew 19:13-15)

A reading from the holy Gospel according
to Matthew
Glory to you, Lord.

The children were brought to Jesus.
He put his hands on them
and he prayed for them.
The disciples tried to stop the people
from bringing the children to Jesus.
But Jesus said,
"Let the children come to me.
Don't stop them!
The kingdom of heaven belongs
to ones such as these."
Jesus then blessed the children.

The Gospel of the Lord.
Praise to you, Lord Jesus Christ.

Responsorial Prayer: Thanks and Praise

Loving God,
Jesus the teacher,
Spirit of wisdom,
you call us again and again
to follow you,
to be your disciples.
All: We give you thanks.
For summer memories,
All: We give you praise.
For your gift of creation,
All: We give you thanks.
For asking us to be your friend,
All: We give you praise.
For leading us in ways of wisdom,
All: We give you thanks.

Closing Prayer

Dear Jesus,
we are your disciples.
This year, lead us, guide us
and teach us.
May we grow in mind, body and soul.
Help us to make kind choices
and take just actions.
When there is sorrow,
help us to comfort.
When there is anger,
help us to bring peace.
When there is joy,
help us celebrate wisely.
When there is success,
help us to be grateful.
We make this prayer
in your loving name.
+ **Amen.**

2. We Follow Jesus

"Come with me!"

(John 1:43)

Opening Prayer

+ Dear Jesus,
You call us to be your friends.
Your amazing love calls us to be true friends
to each other.
Through this school year,
let us walk with you
let us talk with you,
let us pray with you,
and let us be guided by you.
Let us listen to your word calling out to the
disciples.
Amen.

Jesus Calls the Disciples

(Mark 1:16-18)

A reading from the holy Gospel according
to Mark
Glory to you, Lord.

As Jesus walked along the shore of Lake
Galilee, he saw two fishermen, Simon and
his brother Andrew, catching fish with a net.
Jesus said to them, "Come with me, and I
will teach you to catch men." At once they
left their nets and went with him.

The Gospel of the Lord.
Praise to you, Lord Jesus Christ.

Litany: Being Called

Loving Jesus, you still call out to us today
at this school.
All: We say "yes" to your call.

You call us to walk in peace through conflict.
All: We say "yes" to your call.
You call us to speak out against injustice.
All: We say "yes" to your call.
You call us to comfort the sorrowful.
All: We say "yes" to your call.
You call us to bring hope to the despairing.
All: We say "yes" to your call.
You call us to be light in the gloom.
All: We say "yes" to your call.
You call us to heal the hurting.
All: We say "yes" to your call.
You call us to teach the confused.
All: We say "yes" to your call.
You call us to bring the lost home to you.
All: We say "yes" to your call.

Loving Jesus,
every day you call us again to follow you.
Let us always listen to your guiding voice.

Our Father

Jesus taught his disciples to pray
with these words:
All: Our Father …

Closing Prayer

Loving God,
bless us during this school year.
Give us the courage
to answer your call.
Give us the determination
to let your way be our way
this year and every year.
We make this prayer in the name of Jesus,
who is the way, the truth and the life.
+ Amen.

3. Sunflowers

The desert will rejoice,
and flowers will bloom.

(Isaiah 35:1)

Introduction

+ It's amazing to think that within a tiny seed is all that is needed for it to grow into a tall, beautiful sunflower. Each seed must be given water and sunlight to begin its growth. It needs to be planted in good soil. Taking out weeds, adding fertilizer and careful pruning make these big yellow blooms seem to reach for the sun as they tower over the garden.

As children, we also start out very small. Within each of us is the promise of a beautiful grown-up. Each of us, given love and support, begins to grow. We need to live in a healthy environment. By weeding out sin and adding faith and education we shape our personalities and nourish our bodies so that we, too, bloom as we reach for God.

The Bible speaks to us about planting seeds in the right soil.

The Parable of the Sower
(adapted from Matthew 13:3-9, 18-30)

A reading from the holy Gospel according to Matthew
Glory to you, Lord.

Once there was a man who went out to plant seeds. As he scattered the seeds in his field, some of them fell on the path nearby. The birds ate up all those seeds.

Some of the seeds fell onto some rocky ground where there wasn't very much soil. These seeds sprouted quickly, but because there wasn't much soil for the seeds to root deeply, the plants wilted and died when the sun came up.

Some of the plants fell into some thorn bushes. These plants were choked by the surrounding thorns.

Some of the seeds fell on good soil. These plants grew up to be big and strong, and produced more and more seeds.

Jesus tells us that the seeds that fell on the path are like people who hear about God's message but do not understand.

The seeds that fell on the rocky ground are like people who hear about God's message but it doesn't really sink into their hearts. So when trouble comes, they give up too easily.

The seeds that fell into the thorn bushes are like those people who hear about God's message but who care only about their love of riches. The message gets choked out and they will not bear fruit.

But the seeds that fall on good soil are like the people who hear the word of God, understand it and take it to heart. These people will grow up to be true believers. They will bear fruit.

The Gospel of the Lord.
Praise to you, Lord Jesus Christ.

Litany: May We Grow Like a Sunflower

All: May we grow like a sunflower, tall and proud.
With proper care, we can all grow up to be true believers. We need to show the world that we are proud of who we are and proud of our faith.

All: May we grow like a sunflower, bright and beautiful.
Jesus calls us to be the best we can be. When we try our best in everything we do, we are bright and beautiful.

All: May we grow like a sunflower, sharing our gifts for all to see.
We are asked to share our gifts with others. Some of us are good at sports. Some are good at drawing. Others are good at writing stories. Some are good friends. Let's all share our gifts.

All: May we provide food to feed others, like the sunflower does.
We are called to feed others. This does not only mean giving food to the poor, it also means feeding others with kindness and respect.

All: May we grow like a sunflower, reaching for the sun.
As we journey through our lives, we are asked to grow closer to God. We can do this by talking to God every day in prayer. God will hear us and help us to grow. And like the little sunflower seed, we will continue to bloom.

Closing Prayer

God of all,
may we ever grow in faith and love;
may we ever share our gifts with others;
may we ever grow towards you,
like the sunflower and all life on earth.
We ask this through your Son,
our Lord Jesus Christ.
+ Amen.

4. God Gives Us Courage

"Don't be afraid."

(Luke 1:30)

Opening Prayer

+ God of courage,
may we always seek to do what is right, no matter what others say or think.
May we face our fears knowing that you are by our side.
May we honestly try to be the best we can be, each and every day.
We know that we may not
always be brave,
but with your gift of courage,
may we be always willing to try new things as we follow Jesus, your Son,
our model of courage.
Amen.

Let us listen to a story from the Bible about courage given to a young boy named David.

David and Goliath
(adapted from 1 Samuel 17:1-54)

There once were two warring nations: the Israelites and the Philistines. They had been fighting for a very long time. In the camp of the Philistines was a giant named Goliath. Goliath was mean. He was over 3 metres tall and wore bronze armour that weighed about 50 kilograms! He also wore a bronze helmet and carried a bronze javelin over his shoulder. His spear was as thick as his arm. His shield was so large that he had another soldier carry it in front of him when he went into battle.

Goliath shouted at the Israelites, "Choose one of your men to fight me! If he wins (which is unlikely), we Philistines will be your slaves, but if I win, you will be our slaves. I dare you to pick someone!" King Saul of the Israelites was terrified of Goliath. He and his soldiers shook with fear.

In Bethlehem, there lived a boy named David who was the youngest of eight sons born to a man named Jesse. While his older brothers had gone to fight in the war with the Israelites and King Saul, David stayed in Bethlehem and looked after his father's sheep. One day Jesse said to David, "Take these loaves of bread and roasted grains to your brothers at the war front. Take this cheese to the commanding officer. Find out if your brothers are doing all right. There has been news of a terrible giant attacking the Israelites."

So the next morning, David set out for King Saul's camp, taking the food as his father had told him. When he got there, he saw the Israelites and the Philistines lining up for another battle. He left the food with the officer in charge of the supplies and went to find his brothers. While he was talking to them, the giant Goliath came forward and attacked the Israelites as he had done before. When the Israelites saw him, they ran away in fear.

King Saul, dismayed by what he saw, decided to offer a big reward to the man who beat Goliath. David's eldest brother noticed that David had been listening. He got angry with David and said,

"What are you still doing here? Go home and look after the sheep! It's too dangerous for you here! Go home!"

David moved away but he didn't leave. He noticed that nobody was taking the king up on his offer. So he went to the king and declared, "Your Majesty, let me fight Goliath!"

The king replied, "But you are just a boy! What could you do?"

David said, "I look after my father's sheep. Every time a lion or a bear comes, I protect the sheep and get rid of the beasts. If I can do that to lions and bears, I can do this to Goliath. The Lord has saved me from lions and bears. The Lord will give me courage to fight this Philistine. I'm not afraid! I will fight Goliath!"

So King Saul decided to let David fight Goliath. He gave him his own armour and his bronze helmet to wear, too. David tried to put on the king's sword over the armour but he had trouble walking because he wasn't used to wearing armour. Finally David said, "I can't fight in this stuff! I'm not used to it!" So he took it all off. All he had was his shepherd's stick. He bent down and picked up five smooth stones from the ground and got his slingshot ready. Then he set out to meet Goliath.

Goliath started to walk towards David. When the giant got a good look at him and saw that he was only a boy, he began to laugh. "What's that stick for?" he asked. "Do you think I am a dog who wants to play fetch? Come on, then, I will feed your body to the animals and birds to eat!"

David answered, "You are coming against me with armour and a sword, but I come against you with God on my side. Today God gives me courage and strength to defeat you. Everyone will see that the Lord does not need spears or swords to save his people."

They met on the battlefield. Goliath started to run towards David with his weapons outstretched. David reached into his bag and took out one stone. He put it in his slingshot and fired. The stone hit Goliath right in the middle of his forehead. Goliath fell face downwards on the ground. David had beaten Goliath. The war was over.

The word of the Lord.
Thanks be to God.

Litany: God Gives Us Courage

The response is:
God gives us courage.

In the classroom, when we work and play with those who might not be our friends,
All: God gives us courage.
When we are doing what we know is right, even though others are not,
All: God gives us courage.
In the schoolyard, when we need to keep the peace,
All: God gives us courage.
When we make mistakes and we are sorry,
All: God gives us courage.
When we're trying something new,
All: God gives us courage.
When we are scared,
All: God gives us courage.
Always…
All: God gives us courage.
May we always remember that God gives us courage.
+ **Amen.**

5. Jesus Is Our Teacher

Jesus went all over Galilee,
teaching in the synagogues,
[and] preaching the Good News
about the Kingdom.
(*Matthew 4:23*)

Introduction

+ We often hear about Jesus being called "teacher." Today, students see their teacher in their classroom and may wonder why Jesus was called teacher. His classroom and students were very different from our classroom, but as you will see, Jesus was indeed a teacher – the greatest teacher of all.

Mrs. Brown finished taking attendance and told her students to get out their books and begin their lessons.

Most of the students opened their notebooks and started on their task. But as Mrs. Brown's eyes travelled around the classroom, her smile changed to a frown. There in the back row was Joey. Joey did not have his book on his desk and he appeared to be daydreaming.

Mrs. Brown asked him, "Joey, what are you doing? Can't you see the class has begun? Please take out your book!"

Joey looked thoughtful a moment and then said, "I was wondering, Mrs. Brown, why do we call Jesus our teacher? He didn't take attendance or gather his students like you do."

"That's a good question, Joey. Let's put it to the class. Students, why do you think we call Jesus our teacher?"

Sally put up her hand, "Well… Jesus did gather his disciples and he called each one by name (Matthew 4:18-22). He still calls each one of us by name too… right?"

"But what about his classroom? He didn't have one!" Julia insisted.

Mrs. Brown explained, "Sometimes his classroom was in the synagogues (Matthew 4:23). Sometimes he taught from a fishing boat (Matthew 8:23-27). Other times he taught from a mount (Matthew 5:1) or under a grove of olive trees. True, his classroom often had no walls, but wherever he was, Jesus taught the people."

"But he didn't assign any homework or give any tests," declared Marcus.

"Oh, but he *did* give assignments," said Philip. "Don't you remember? He told the people to love God and to love one another (Matthew 22:34-40). He told them to feed the hungry, clothe the naked, and visit the sick and those in prison. He even told them to share their money with the poor (Matthew 25:35-40)."

"Whoa, that's a big assignment!" said Joey.

"But just a minute … He didn't mark papers or give out any grades, did he?" asked Carol.

Mrs. Brown answered, "It's true that he didn't assign grades for report cards, but he did explain that each person would be judged at the end of their time to see if they fulfilled their assigned tasks (Matthew 25:45-46)."

"OK, OK … but what about recess duty or watching his students have their lunch like other teachers? Jesus didn't do any of these," stated William.

"He fed thousands and watched them eat," said Mrs. Brown. He prayed over them. Jesus was always watching over his followers. He still watches over us today (Matthew 28:20)."

The class suddenly became very quiet. "So, Joey, does all this answer your question?" asked Mrs. Brown.

Joey looked up at Mrs. Brown. "Yeah … thanks for answering, Mrs. Brown. I guess you were right. Jesus is our teacher and we learn from him every day. He's the greatest teacher of all."

Litany: Jesus Our Teacher

When we don't know which way to go, we know we can follow you.

All: Jesus, You are our leader.
When we have questions, we know that you have the answers.
All: Jesus, You are our answer.
When we worship, we praise your name.
All: Jesus, You are our Lord.
When we live our lives, we look to you for guidance.
All: Jesus, you are our leader, our answer, our Lord.
Jesus, you are our teacher.
Teach us to follow your example. Amen.

Let us close this prayer service by praying the prayer that Jesus the Teacher taught us:
All: Our Father …
+ Amen.

October

1. God Is in You

So God created human beings,
making them to be like himself.

(Genesis 1:27)

Opening Reflection: God Is in You!

+ [Left side: *Right side*]
When your friends look at you …
They can see God.
When your classmates look at you …
They can see God.
When your teachers look at you …
They can see God.
When your family looks at you …
They can see God.
For God is in you.

[*Right side:* Left side]
When you look at your friends …
you can see God.
When you look at your classmates …
you can see God.
When you look at your teachers …
you can see God.
When you look at your family …
you can see God.
For God is in them, too.

All: Each of us has been made
in the image of God.
Help us, O God, to see you
in others and in ourselves.
We ask this in the name of Jesus,
our brother.
Amen.

Made in God's Image

(Genesis 1:26-31)

A reading from the Book of Genesis

Then God said, "And now we will make human beings; they will be like us and resemble us. They will have power over the fish, the birds, and all animals, domestic and wild, large and small."

He created them male and female, blessed them, and said, "Have many children, so that your descendants will live all over the earth and bring it under your control. I am putting you in charge of the fish, the birds, and all the wild animals. I have provided all kinds of grain and all kinds of fruit for you to eat …."

God looked at everything he had made and he was very pleased.

The word of the Lord.
Thanks be to God.

Primary Litany: God is in You!
Young and old,
girl or boy,
you are God's special joy.

Black or white,
big or small,
God is in you, one and all.

Math or gym,
read or write,
you are precious in God's sight.

Every colour, every hue,
everybody,
God is in you!

Junior Litany: God is in You!

You may like math or gym
or singing music notes,
or you might enjoy painting pictures
or sailing free on boats,
or perhaps you prefer playing hockey
or writing or reading books,
or maybe acting or trying recipes like your
favourite cooks
but whatever your gifts,
you were born to
develop them and grow,
and God will always see you through.
Remember, all you need to do is
just live your life loving God,
for God is in you.

No matter what language you speak,
or how you do your hair,
no matter if you run, roll or walk,
Or what type of clothes you wear,
whatever you are,
you were born to develop and grow,
and God will always see you through.
Remember, all you need to do is
just live your life loving God,
for God is in you.
Amen.

Closing Prayer

We were all made in the image of God.
God loves us, his creation.
May we always remember
that God is in all of us.
May we always love God.
We ask this through Jesus, our brother.
+ Amen.

2. We Give Thanks

Give thanks to the Lord.
(Psalm 105:1)

Opening Prayer

+ Gracious God,
As leaves turn to gold,
you shine with your goodness.

We give thanks
for all of your good gifts.
Make our hearts even more grateful.
May we also shine with your love.
All: Amen.

God's Creation

(Psalm 104:24-25)

A reading from the Book of Psalms

How many are your works, O God!
In wisdom you made them all;
the earth is full of your creatures.
There is the sea, vast and spacious,
teeming with creatures beyond number,
living things both large and small.

The word of the Lord.
Thanks be to God.

Litany: Gratitude

In this season of falling leaves
and cooling temperatures,
we draw closer to you.
All: We thank you, God.
For sun-bright days and rain-soaked nights,
All: We thank you, God.
For gold-brown leaves and fading flowers,
All: We thank you, God.
For faithful friends and loving families,
All: We thank you, God.
For caring teachers and devoted priests,
All: We thank you, God.
For joyful music and thinking games,
All: We thank you, God.
For all good things and all good times,
All: We thank you, God.

Closing Prayer

God of seasons of splendour,
we praise your gracious gifts.
Again and again
we give you our thanks.

May our thanksgiving
lead us to give
of our own gifts and talents.
We make this prayer
in the name of Jesus.
+ **Amen.**

3. Compassion

*"Be merciful
just as your Father is merciful."*
(*Luke 6:36*)

Opening Prayer

+ God of compassion,
help us to show kindness and concern
for others.
Help us to truly listen
and try to assist others
when they need it.
We know that this brings us
closer to you.
Amen.

The Bible speaks to us about compassion.

Love Your Enemies
(adapted from Luke 6:31-36)

A reading from the holy Gospel according
to Luke
Glory to you, Lord.

Do for others what you want them to do
for you. If you love only the people who
love you, why should you receive a special
blessing? Even wicked people love those
who love them. And if you do good only
to those who do good to you, why should
you receive a blessing? Again, even wicked
people do that! And if you lend only to
those you expect will give it back, why
should you receive a blessing? Even wicked
ones lend to wicked people to get back the
same amount!

No! Love your enemies and do good to
them; lend and expect nothing back. You
will then have a great reward and you will
be children of the Most High God. For he
is good to the ungrateful and the wicked.
Be merciful just as your God is merciful.

The Gospel of the Lord.
Praise to you, Lord Jesus Christ.

Compassion Prayer

C is for caring for all people as we should.
O is for outreach to others in our
neighbourhood.
M is for the good manners we show.
P is for our daily prayers, which help our
faith to grow.
A is for acting on what we say.
S is for sharing our gifts each and every day.
S is for singing praises to our God above.
I is for investing time in faith and love.
O is for being open with nothing to hide.
N is for needing compassion far and wide.
Amen.

Closing Reflection

Jesus gave us a new commandment
to love one another as he has loved us.
Compassion means caring:
our friends will know
that no matter what,
they can depend on us.
So when you're in the classroom
or in the schoolyard today,
remember that showing compassion
brings you closer to God.
+ Amen.

4. Through the Eyes of God

God looked at everything he had made,
and he was very pleased.

(Genesis 1:31)

Opening Reflection

+ Imagine, if we could see through the eyes of God, what would we see?

Through the eyes of God, we would see that no matter how old we become, we are all God's children.

Through the eyes of God, we would see that no matter our colour, race or creed, we are all part of the same loving family.

Through the eyes of God, we would see that no matter what our differences are, keeping the peace is always important.

Through the eyes of God, we would see that no matter what our individual gifts, it is wonderful when we share them and use them for the good of all.

If we could look into the eyes of God, we would see our reflection mirrored in his loving gaze as he looked back at us.

The Bible speaks to us about what God sees.

A Song of Praise
(adapted from Psalm 33)

A reading from the Book of Psalms

The Lord looks down from heaven
and sees all of us humans.
From where he rules, he looks down
on all those who live on earth.
He sees all our thoughts
and knows everything that we do.

The Lord watches over those
who obey him.
He looks out for those who trust
in his constant love.
He saves all his people from evil and
he keeps us safe and in peace in times of
trouble.

The love of the Lord is constant.

The word of the Lord.
Thanks be to God.

Litany: God Looks on Us with Love

The eyes of God watched over us when we took our first breath, took our first steps and said our first word.
All: God looks on us with love.

The eyes of God watched over us when we entered the Church through our baptism and when we have gone to Mass with our families.
All: God looks on us with love.

The eyes of God watched over us when we went to school for the first time and made our first friends.
All: God looks on us with love.

The eyes of God watched over us when we learned to write our names and read our first book.
All: God looks on us with love.

The eyes of God will always watch over us lovingly keeping us safe.
All: God will always look on us with love.
+ Amen.

5. Halloween: Deliver Us from Evil

"Keep us safe from the Evil One."
(Matthew 6:13)

Introduction

+ On Halloween, we dress up in costumes of every kind and we laugh in the face of evil. We know that with God on our side, we can face anything. Every time we pray the Lord's Prayer, we say: "Deliver us from evil." May we always turn away from what is not good and turn towards the Kingdom of God.

The Bible speaks to us about trusting God to deliver us from evil.

A Tree and Its Fruit
(adapted from Matthew 7:15-20)

A reading from the holy Gospel according to Matthew
Glory to you, Lord.

"Watch out for those who pretend to be something that they are not. They may come to you acting like they are your friend but really they are not. You will be able to tell who they are by what they do. Like thorn bushes that cannot bear grapes, these people can't be true friends to others. A kind person cannot be mean but will be kind, just like a healthy tree cannot grow bad fruit but will grow only good fruit. A mean person is often mean, just like an unhealthy tree produces bad fruit. Ask the Lord to deliver you from evil and pretenders. Then you will know what to do when false people come to you."

The Gospel of the Lord.
Praise to you, Lord Jesus Christ.

Litany: Deliver Us from Evil

On this All Hallows Eve, or Halloween, we ask God to help us to turn away from situations that could lead us in the wrong direction. We ask God to lead us to goodness and keep us safe from harm.

The response is: **Lead us from temptation and deliver us from evil.**

From the goblins that haunt us,
Lead us from temptation and deliver us from evil.

From the tricky and those we do not trust,
Lead us from temptation and deliver us from evil.

From the unknown darkness of the night,
Lead us from temptation and deliver us from evil.

From the hidden attics of secrets people keep,
Lead us from temptation and deliver us from evil.

From shadowy webs of lies,
Lead us from temptation and deliver us from evil.

From the masks that people hide behind,
Lead us from temptation and deliver us from evil.

From the cauldrons of hatred and meanness,
Lead us from temptation and deliver us from evil.

From the ghosts of broken promises,
**Lead us from temptation and deliver us
from evil.**

From the scarecrows of loneliness,
**Lead us from temptation and deliver us
from evil.**

From the spooky things that frighten us,
**Lead us from temptation and deliver us
from evil.**

This Halloween and always, Lord,
lead us away from temptation
and deliver us from evil,
for the kingdom on earth
and heaven are yours.
Amen.

Closing Prayer

Let us close by praying the prayer that Jesus
taught us:
Our Father ...
+ Amen.

November

1. We Pray with the Saints: All Saints Day

*Ever since I heard of your faith
in the Lord Jesus
and your love for all of God's people,
I have not stopped
giving thanks to God for you.*
(Ephesians 1:15-16)

Opening Prayer

+ God of all time and all space,
we thank you and we praise you.
Together with all the saints,
all good and holy people,
we are joined together
by your goodness, truth and wisdom.
We also give thanks
for all those holy men and women
who shine with their living examples
of your faith, hope and love.
This we pray in Jesus' name.
Amen.

You Are God's Saints

(adapted from Colossians 3:12-15)

A reading from the letter of Paul to
the Colossians

You are God's chosen people.
You are God's saints.
God loves you.
You should be clothed in compassion, kind-
ness, humility,
gentleness and patience.
Be patient and forgiving.
Jesus has forgiven you,
so now you must do the same.
Over all these clothes,
to keep them together
and complete them, put on love.

And may the peace of Christ
reign in your hearts,
because it is for this that you were called
together as parts of one body.

The word of the Lord.
Thanks be to God.

Litany of the Saints

With all of the saints, we pray that God may
continue to bless us.
Lord, have mercy.
All: Lord, have mercy.
Christ, have mercy.
All: Christ, have mercy.
Lord, have mercy.
All: Lord, have mercy.
Christ, hear us.
All: Christ, hear us.
Christ, graciously hear us.
All: Christ, graciously hear us.
Creator God,
All: Have mercy on us.
Jesus Christ,
All: Have mercy on us.
Holy Spirit,
All: Have mercy on us.
Holy Trinity, One God,
All: Have mercy on us.
Mary, Queen of the Apostles,
All: Have mercy on us.
St. Joseph and St. Anne,
patron saints of Canada,
All: Pray for us.
St. Paul the apostle,
patron of evangelists,
All: Pray for us.

St. Thomas Aquinas,
patron saints of students,
All: Pray for us.
St. Francis of Assisi,
patron of ecology,
All: Pray for us.
St. Gregory,
patron of teachers,
All: Pray for us.

_____,
patron of our school,
All: Pray for us.
All you saints of God,
All: Pray for us.

Closing Prayer

Holy God,
through the arms of your saints,
you embrace the whole world
in your love.
May we always know
that we belong to you,
that our true home is among the saints,
and that we are a blessed people
among other blessed people.
We make this prayer
in the name of Jesus.
+ Amen.

2. A Time for Peace

Blessed are those who work for peace.
(Matthew 5:9)

Opening Prayer

+ God of peace,
Help us to live in harmony
with our neighbours.
Teach us to trust in your guidance.
Lead us to your peace.
We ask this through Jesus your Son.
Amen.

God's Peace
(Philippians 4:6-7)

Don't worry about anything, but in all your prayers ask God for what you need, always asking him with a thankful heart. And God's peace, which is far beyond human understanding, will keep your hearts and minds safe in union with Christ Jesus.

The word of the Lord.
Thanks be to God.

Reflections on Peace

Peace is a gift that Jesus gives us. When he appeared to his friends the disciples he would say, "Peace be with you."

This is a greeting that puts everyone at ease.

During Mass, we offer each other the sign of peace. This means that we wish those around us will share in the peace of Christ.

At the end of every Mass, the priest or deacon directs us to "Go in peace to love and serve the Lord." We are called to live in peace with and to love our neighbours.

Too often in our world today, people try to solve their problems with fighting.

We must remember that we are all members of the family of God, and that God wants us, his children, to live in peace.

Ritual

Let us offer each other a sign of peace.

Closing Prayer

God of peace and justice,
in our classrooms
and in our school today,
we ask you to help us
to be mindful of treating each other
with respect
and to keep the peace
in our little corner of the world.
We ask this through your Son Jesus,
our friend.
+ Amen.

3. We Remember

Peace be with you.
(John 20:26)

Opening Prayer

+ Loving God,
hear our prayers today:
prayers of sadness that remember
men, women, girls and boys
who have died in war;
prayers of thanksgiving
for the courage of those
who have been peacemakers;
prayers of hope for a world
where war is a distant memory.
Kindly hear these prayers
and lead us closer to your heart.
This we pray in the name of Jesus.
Amen.

Making Peace
(adapted from Isaiah 2:4)

A reading from the book of the Prophet Isaiah

God will judge between the nations
and will settle conflicts
between many people.
Then they will beat their weapons of war
into tools for peace.
Nation will no longer fight nation,
nor will they prepare for war anymore.

The word of the Lord.
Thanks be to God.

Prayer for Justice and Peace

Let us pray in silence for 2 minutes. We pray
for those who have died in war and other
conflicts.

(2 minutes of silence)
God of courage,
All: Bring peace to the violent.
God of comfort,
All: Bring healing to the hurting.
God of wisdom,
All: Bring justice to the wronged.
God of love,
All: Bring hope to the despairing.
We pray that our classrooms,
schools and communities
will always remember
to be places of peace and justice.

Hail Mary

We pray with Mary, who knew what it was
to lose a son to a violent death.
Hail Mary …

Closing Prayer

God of peace and justice,
guide our hands and hearts
to make our world full of
peaceful places:
homes of hope and warmth,
schools of safety and caring,
parishes of welcome and reverence,
communities of creativity and respect,
countries of justice and freedom,
continents of harmony and unity,
and a world where humans take their
rightful place as nature's guardians.
We make this prayer in the name of Jesus,
Prince of Peace.
+ Amen.

4. The Golden Rule: The Good Samaritan

"Do for others just what you want them to do for you."
(Luke 6:31)

Introduction

+ We know that we need to treat others as we would like to be treated; this is what we call the Golden Rule. Sometimes, if a person isn't one of our good friends, we find this hard to do and we aren't as nice as we could be. Jesus asks us to treat everyone as our neighbour, including those we may not like very much.

Jesus speaks to us about the Golden Rule.

The Good Samaritan
(adapted from Luke 10:29-37)

A reading from the holy Gospel according to Luke
Glory to you, Lord.

A teacher of the Law asked Jesus:
"Who is my neighbour?"

Jesus answered, "There was once a Jewish man who was going down the road from Jerusalem to Jericho when robbers attacked him, stripped him and beat him up, leaving him for dead.

"It so happened that later on that day, a priest was going down that same road. When he saw the man who had been attacked, he walked on by, on the other side of the road.

"Soon a Levite was also walking down that same road. He went over and looked at the man and then, like the priest, he walked on by, on the other side of the road.

"Finally, a Samaritan who was also travelling down the same road came upon the man. Samaritans did not usually speak to Jewish people, for normally they did not get along, but when he saw the man who had been attacked, his heart was filled with pity. He went over to the man, bandaged and cleaned his wounds, put him on his own donkey and took him to an inn, where he took care of him.

"The next day, the Samaritan took out some money and gave it to the innkeeper, telling him to take care of the man. He also said that he would pay for any other extra expenses when he came by the inn again."

Jesus concluded, "In your opinion, which of these three followed the golden rule and so acted like a neighbour towards the man who was attacked by robbers?"

The teacher of the Law answered, "The one who was kind to him, of course."

Jesus replied, "You go, then, and do the same."

The Gospel of the Lord.
Praise to you, Lord Jesus Christ.

Litany: The Golden Rule

God of fairness,
we look to your Son, Jesus,
to show us how to treat others
equally and honestly,
for we know that we also
want to be treated with fairness.
All: Jesus, teach us to treat others fairly.

God of kindness,
we look to your Son, Jesus,
to show us how to be caring
and considerate to everyone we meet,
for we know that this is the way
to your kingdom.
All: Jesus, teach us to be always kind.

God of justice,
we look to your Son, Jesus,
to show us how to act with honesty
and generosity,
for we know that this is the only way
to live justly.
All: Jesus, teach us to live with justice.

God of all,
teach us to always treat others
as we ourselves would like to be treated,
for we know that this is the true way
to your Kingdom.
We ask this through your Son,
Jesus Christ.
+ Amen.

5. We Seek Justice

*If you listen to me, you will know
what is right, just and fair.*

(Proverbs 2:9)

Opening Prayer

+ God of justice,

We know that we should always work hard
to treat others with respect and fairness.
Help us to remember to play by the rules
and to take turns. Teach us to live with justice every day, so we can live happily with
others and look for peaceful solutions to any
problems. We ask this through your Son,
our Saviour Jesus Christ.
Amen.

The Bible speaks to us about justice and
playing fairly and by the rules.

Playing Fair

(adapted from 2 Timothy 2:3-6)

A reading from the second letter of Paul
to Timothy

An athlete who runs in a race will not win
the prize if she doesn't follow the rules. The
only way for a farmer to succeed is to work
hard all season and then his harvest will be
great. Think about this and the Lord God
will help you to understand.

The word of the Lord.
Thanks be to God.

The Bible speaks to us about justice and
treating others with respect.

The Golden Rule

(adapted from Luke 6:29-31, 34-35)

A reading from the holy Gospel according
to Luke
Glory to you, Lord.

"If someone takes your coat, let him have
your shirt as well. Give to everyone who
asks you for something, and when someone
takes what is yours, do not ask for it back.
Do for others just what you want them to
do for you. Lend your things to others and
expect nothing back. Love your enemies
and be good to them. Then you will be truly
blessed as children of God."

The Gospel of the Lord.
Praise to you, Lord Jesus Christ.

The Bible talks to us about justice, mercy
and peace:

True Happiness

(adapted from Matthew 5:7-9)

A reading from the holy Gospel according
to Matthew
Glory to you, Lord.

Happy are those who show mercy to others;
God will be merciful to them.
Happy are those who are pure in heart;
they will see God.
Happy are those who work for peace;
God will call them his children.

The Gospel of the Lord.
Praise to you, Lord Jesus Christ.

The Bible talks to us about justice and peaceful solutions.

Peace and Justice
(adapted from Micah 4:2-4)

God teaches us what he wants us to do. If we follow his Word, and will walk the path he has chosen, then God will settle all the arguments among the nations. They will change their weapons into plows for farming and their spears into tools. Countries will never again go to war and battle each other. Everyone will live in peace and live on their own land. No one will make them afraid. The Lord Almighty has promised this.

The word of the Lord.
Thanks be to God.

Petitions:

The response is: **May we seek justice, O God.**
We seek to play fair in the classroom and in our schoolyard games.
May we seek justice, O God.
We seek to treat others as we want to be treated.
May we seek justice, O God.
We seek to respect people from other nations and faiths.
May we seek justice, O God.
We seek peace in our school life and in our community.
May we seek justice, O God.
+ **Amen.**

December

1. Advent I: Find Hope

God fills us with a living hope.
(1 Peter 1:3)

Ritual: Lighting the First Advent Candle

+ As the days become darker, we begin the Advent season and light the first candle of our Advent wreath. Let us light the way in the darkness and make straight the path to God. We await the coming of our Saviour with hope.

Opening Prayer

God of light, bring us hope.
Help us to find hope this Advent season.
Help us to prepare
for the coming of the Lord.
We make this prayer
in the name of Jesus, our hope.
Amen.

The Future King
(Isaiah 9:2-3, 6-7)

A reading from the Book of the Prophet Isaiah

The people who walked in darkness
have seen a great light.
They lived in a land of shadows,
but now light is shining on them.
You have given them great joy, Lord; you
have made them happy.
They rejoice in what you have done,
as people rejoice
when they harvest grain
or when they divide captured wealth.

A child is born to us!
A son is given to us!

And he will be our ruler.
He will be called,
"Wonderful Counsellor,"
"Mighty God," "Eternal Father,"
"Prince of Peace."
His royal power will continue to grow;
his kingdom will always be at peace.
He will rule as King David's successor,
basing his power on right and justice,
from now until the end of time.
The Lord Almighty is determined
to do all this.

The word of the Lord.
Thanks be to God.

What Is Hope?

Hope let us see God's light ahead of us.
Hope opens our hearts to dream.
Hope looks forward to promises and new possibilities.
Hope is eternal and everlasting.

Hope
Offers us the true
Promise of Christ
Eternally, forever.

Closing Prayer

God of hope,
guide us in your way
this Advent and always.
Let us put our trust
in your gentle hands
as we look forward to the birth
of your Son, our Saviour.
We ask this in hope through
Christ our Lord.
+ **Amen.**

2. Advent II: Find Faith

Happy is the person who remains faithful.
(James 1:12)

Ritual: Lighting the First and Second Advent Candles

+ In this second week of Advent, let us light the first two candles of our Advent wreath. We await the coming of our Lord Jesus and light the way to see the face of God. We follow the light of God with faith and hope.

Opening Prayer

God of light, bring us faith.
Help us to find faith this Advent.
Help us to prepare
for the coming of the Lord.
We make this prayer in the name of Jesus
your Son, source of our faith. **Amen.**

What Is Faith?

Faith joins us as a family
and brings us together.
Faith is belief in our loving God.
Faith brings comfort
in times of trouble and in times of joy.
Faith brings heaven closer to us.

Faith is the
Answer
In both bad
Times and good; we thank our
Heavenly Father for faith.

The Angel Gabriel Visits Mary
(Luke 1:28-35, 38)

A reading from the holy Gospel according to Luke
Glory to you, Lord.

The angel came to Mary and said, "Peace be with you! The Lord is with you and has greatly blessed you!"

Mary was deeply troubled by the angel's message, and she wondered what his words meant. The angel said to her, "Don't be afraid, Mary; You will become pregnant and will give birth to a son, and you will name him Jesus. He will be great and will be called the Son of the Most High God. The Lord God will make him a king, as his ancestor David was, and he will be the king of the descendants of Jacob forever; his kingdom will never end!"

Mary said to the angel, "I am a virgin. How, then, can this be?"

The angel answered, "The Holy Spirit will come on you, and God's power will rest upon you. For this reason the holy child will be called the Son of God."

"I am the Lord's servant," said Mary; "may it happen to me as you have said." The Gospel of the Lord.
Praise to you, Lord Jesus Christ.

Closing Prayer

Faithful God,
guide us in your way
this Advent and always.
As we look forward
to the birth of your Son,
May our faith grow stronger
with every passing day.
We ask this through
Christ, our Lord.
+ Amen.

3. Advent III: Find Joy

When they saw the [same star] how happy they were, what joy was theirs!
(Matthew 2:10)

Ritual: Lighting the First, Second and Third Advent Candles

+ In this third week of Advent, let us light the first three candles in our Advent wreath. We light the way out of the darkness to see the light of God. We walk the path to God with joy, faith and hope.

Opening Prayer

God of light, bring us joy.
Help us to find joy this Advent.
Help us to prepare
for the coming of the Lord.
We make this prayer in the name of Jesus,
our Joy.
Amen.

Mary's Song of Praise
(Luke 1:46-55)

A reading from the holy Gospel according to Luke
Glory to you, Lord.

Mary said,
"My heart praises the Lord.;
my soul is glad
because of God my Saviour,
for he has remembered me,
his lowly servant!
From now on,
all people will call me happy,
because of the great things
the Mighty God has done for me.

God's name is holy;
from one generation to another
he shows mercy
to those who honour him.
He has stretched out his mighty arm
and scattered the proud
with all their plans.
He has brought down mighty kings
from their thrones
and lifted up the lowly.
He has filled the hungry with good things
and sent the rich away
with empty hands.
He has kept the promise
he made to our ancestors,
and has come to the help
of his servant Israel.
He has remembered to show mercy
to Abraham and to all his
descendants forever!"

The Gospel of the Lord.
Praise to you, Lord Jesus Christ.

What Is Joy?

Joy is the delightful anticipation we sense all around us this season.
Joy is the happy fullness that our hearts feel at the news of the coming of Jesus.
Joy is the feeling of wonder shared by young and old alike who will welcome the Son of God into their hearts.

J is the happy feeling that both
Old and
Young share during Advent.

Response Prayer

The response is:
Let us be filled with joy.
When we greet each other in the hallways,
Let us be filled with joy.
When we work together in our classrooms,
Let us be filled with joy.
When we play with our friends in the
schoolyard,
Let us be filled with joy.
When we share a smile with others, **Let us
be filled with joy.**
When we spend time with our families this
Christmas,
Let us be filled with joy.
When we prepare our hearts to receive Jesus,
Let us be filled with joy.

Let us be filled with joy
this Christmas season and always.
Amen.

Closing Prayer

God of joy,
guide us in your way this Advent
and always.
As we draw closer to the
cradle of your Son Jesus,
fill us with joy and wonder.
We ask this through Christ our Lord.
+ Amen.

4. Advent IV: Find Love

"You are my own dear Son.
I am pleased with you."

(Luke 3:22)

Ritual: Lighting All Four Advent Candles

+ This is the fourth week of Advent. Our wait is almost over. As we light the four Advent candles, we await the coming of Emmanuel with love, joy, faith and hope.

Opening Prayer

God of light, bring us love.
Help us to find love this Advent.
Help us to prepare
for the coming of the Lord.
We make this prayer
in the name of Jesus,
our loving Lord.
Amen.

Mary Visits Elizabeth
(Luke 1:39-45)

A reading from the holy Gospel according to Luke.
Glory to you, Lord.

Mary got ready and hurried off to a town in the hill country of Judea. She went into Zechariah's house and greeted [her cousin] Elizabeth. When Elizabeth heard Mary's greeting, the baby moved within her. Elizabeth was filled with the Holy Spirit and said in a loud voice, "You are the most blessed of all women, and blessed is the child that you will bear! Why should this great thing happen to me, that my Lord's mother comes to visit me? For as soon as I heard your greeting, the baby within me jumped with gladness. How happy you are to believe that the Lord's message to you will come true!"

The Gospel of the Lord.
Praise to you, Lord Jesus Christ.

What Is Love?

Love is the warmth we share
with our families and friends.
Love comes from our hearts and souls.
Love is vital, valuable
and important to our lives.
True love is eternal
and never fades away.

Love
Opens our hearts and is
Vital to our
Everlasting happiness

Closing Prayer

Loving God,
Guide us in your way
this Advent and always.
May we put ourselves
in your loving arms
as we look forward to the birth
of your Son, our Saviour.
We ask this in love through
Christ our Lord.
+ Amen.

5. Bless Our Gifts: An Advent Charity Drive

"Give to others, and God will give to you ..."
(Luke 6:38)

Opening Prayer

+ God of all that is good and holy,
bless the gifts that we have collected
for those in need.
Bless them with hope and strength.
May these gifts
help them on their journeys.
As you care for us,
help us on our journeys, too.
We make this prayer in Jesus' name.
Amen.

The Early Christians Share Their Gifts
(Acts 2:42-46)

A reading from the Acts of the Apostles

They spent their time in learning from the
apostles, taking part in the fellowship, and
sharing in the fellowship and the prayers.
Many miracles and wonders were being
done through the apostles and everyone was
filled with awe.

All the believers continued together in close
fellowship and shared their belongings with
one another. They would sell their property
and possessions, and distribute the money
among all, according to what each one
needed. Day after day they met as a group
in the Temple, and they had their meals together in their homes, eating with glad and
humble hearts, praising God, and enjoying
the good will of all the people.

The word of the Lord.
Thanks be to God.

Blessing of the Gifts

Loving God,
may our gifts be pleasing to you.
Make our homes, school,
and community
places of blessing this Advent season.

God of hope and generosity,
we await Christmas
and we prepare our hearts.
We give thanks for the gifts before us.
All: We bless these gifts.
We give thanks to those
who gave these gifts.
**All: We bless those
who gave these gifts.**
We give thanks for those
who organized this drive.
**All: We bless those
who organized this drive.**
We pray for those
who will receive these gifts.
**All: We bless those
who will receive these gifts.**

Closing Prayer

Loving God,
we thank you
and bless your holy name.
May this Advent action help prepare our
hearts and our world
for the celebration of your birth
at Christmas.
We make this prayer
in the name of Jesus,
Prince of Peace.
+ **Amen.**

January

1. A New Hope, A New Year

*Praise the Lord,
all living creatures!*

(*Psalm 150:6*)

Opening Prayer

+ God of time and space,
God of the universe,
God of creation,
Bless this new year.
May we use the gifts of time
and the gifts of our lives
to continue to do your work.
Let us be mirrors of your light
and your compassion;
Let us make our hearts and homes sacred
places in this sacred time.
We make this prayer
in the name of Jesus.
Amen.

Sing a New Song
(Psalm 95)

A reading from the Book of Psalms

O sing a new song to the Lord,
sing to the Lord all the earth.
O sing to the Lord, bless his name.
Proclaim his help day by day.
Let the heavens rejoice
and earth be glad,
let the sea and all within it
thunder praise
let the land and all it bears rejoice.
All the trees of the wood shout for joy
at the presence of the Lord
for he comes,
he comes to rule the earth.

With justice he will rule the world,
he will judge the peoples with his truth.

The word of the Lord.
Thanks be to God.

A Litany for the New Year

Loving God,

you bless this hour,
this day, this new year.
Let us give thanks for this gift.

In our learning and leisure,
All: Walk with us this year.
In our hurting and healing,
All: Walk with us this year.
In our celebration and sorrows,
All: Walk with us this year.
To the poor and the neglected,
All: Walk with us this year.
To our homes and our churches,
All: Walk with us this year.

Our Father

Jesus taught us a special prayer to guide us
through each day.
Our Father …

Closing Prayer

Loving God,
in this time and space,
we praise and bless you
as you bless our time together.
Continue to bless us with your love
throughout the year.
We make this prayer
in the name of Jesus.
+ **Amen.**

2. Unity: We Are One Body

We are one body
in union with Christ.

(*Romans 12:5*)

Introduction

+ We are united in the Body of Christ. This means that we are all children of God and so we are to make everyone feel welcome and appreciated. As members of God's family, we should always use our words to help and not to hurt. Unity means togetherness in God.

The Bible speaks to us about unity.

One Body with Many Members

(adapted from 1 Corinthians 12:12-21, 26-27)

A reading from the first letter of Paul to the Corinthians

Just as each of us has one body with many parts so are we all parts of the one Body in Christ. When we were baptized we were all joined together and united as one family in God.

Think about your own bodies. Would your foot say "Because I am not a hand, I do not belong to the body?" Or would your ear say, "Because I am not an eye, I do not belong to the body?" Of course not, because they all belong.

All the parts belong even though they are different from each other. If your whole body was an eye, how could you hear? Or if your whole body was an ear, how would you be able to smell anything?

God has arranged all of the parts of our bodies in the way He chose. God has arranged all the parts of the Body of Christ in the way He chose too. Each member is important and has their own job to do.

So the eye can't say to the hand, "I do not need you." Or the head can't say to the feet, "I do not need you." We all need each other to grow.

So if one part suffers, the whole body suffers. If one part is honoured, the whole body is honoured.

Now we are all individually members of the Body of Christ. We are all different. Some of us are teachers. Others are learners. Some of us are healers. Others are peacemakers. Some of us are leaders. Some of us follow. We are all different but we all belong. We are all united in the Body of Christ.

The word of the Lord.
Thanks be to God.

How We See Unity in Our School

Alone we are not as strong as a community that helps one another. When heavy loads are carried alone, they can be difficult to lift.

When we are united and help each other together to grow, we are much stronger people because unity means that we work together.

When we are alone, we can often be easily broken.

But like twigs bound together, it is more difficult to break our spirits.

When we work together, we are more successful. When we are united, we all grow closer to God.

We are children of faith who follow the example of Christ. Jesus told us that when we value all people around us as members of God's family, we show our love for Jesus. Unity means that we always remember – whether we're in the classroom or in the schoolyard or at home – that we are to make everyone feel welcome and appreciated. Unity means that together we grow, in Jesus' name.

+ **Amen.**

3. The Kindness of God's People

For this very reason do your best
to add goodness to your faith.

(2 Peter 1:5)

Opening Prayer

+ God of kindness,
you touch our hearts
with your warmth and light.
May we be warmth and light
to our friends and families.
When there is suffering, let us comfort;
when there is pain, let us heal;
and when there is loneliness let us be a
friend.
We make this prayer
in the name of Jesus Christ
who is God's kindness.
Amen.

Be Imitators of God
(Ephesians 5:1-2)

A reading from the letter of Paul
to the Ephesians

Be imitators of God, therefore,
as dearly loved children
and live a life of love,
just as Christ loved us
and gave himself up for us
as a fragrant offering
and sacrifice to God.

The word of the Lord.
Thanks be to God.

Litany: Kindness

Jesus is our model of kindness.
It is Jesus who told us,
"Be compassionate
as I am compassionate."
Loving God,
open our hearts and our souls
to the broken-hearted.
All: Let us bring your kindness.
To those who are ill,
All: Let us bring your kindness.
To those who are excluded,
All: Let us bring your kindness.
To those who suffer injustice,
All: Let us bring your kindness.
To those who are hungry,
All: Let us bring your kindness.
To those who are suffering
because of war,
All: Let us bring your kindness.
To all those in need of your love,
All: Let us bring your kindness.

Closing Prayer

Kind and loving God,
bless all of us who are in special need
of your kindness.
Bless all those who are striving
to be kind.
Teach us to increase
our caring and commitment,
to become closer to the way
we need to be,
to make our classrooms and homes
communities of kindness.
We make this prayer
in the name of Jesus.
+ **Amen.**

4. Prayers of Comfort at a Time of Loss

Comfort my people,
says our God.

(Isaiah 40:1)

Opening Prayer

+ Healing God,
our hearts are saddened
by painful news.
Comfort our friend,
comfort the family,
comfort all of us.
Open our hearts
so that we hear your words today.
Amen.

Scriptural Comfort

Let us meditate prayerfully on these lines
from scripture:

"Be still and know that I am God."
(Psalm 46:10)

"Comfort, O comfort my people."
(Isaiah 40)

"Even though I walk through the
darkest valley, I fear no evil."
(Psalm 23:4)

"Blessed are those who mourn,
for they will be comforted."
(Matthew 5:4)

Litany: Comfort and Peace

God of comfort and peace,
you know our sorrow.
Bless these people for whom we now pray:
For _____, who
left this world and is now in your loving
embrace.
All: We pray to the Lord.
For _____, our friend
who needs our support and care.
All: We pray to the Lord.

For our friend's family, that they may know
that beyond tears lies your peace.
All: We pray to the Lord.

For all of our own losses – relatives and
friends – that we may also feel God's warmth.
All: We pray to the Lord.

Hail Mary

We ask for the prayers of Mary in this time
of sorrow:
Hail Mary ...

Closing Prayer

Caring God,
give us strength and hope
to meet the challenges in front of us.
May we be your voice of comfort,
your hands of peace,
and your heart of love,
today and always.
This we pray in the name of Jesus.
+ Amen.

5. St. Thomas Aquinas: Patron Saint of Catholic Schools

"I am the first, the last,
the only God."

(Isaiah 44:6)

Introduction

+ Today we celebrate St. Thomas Aquinas who is the patron saint of Catholic schools and students. Thomas was born to a wealthy family in Italy around the year 1225. He was very intelligent but because he was large and very quiet, many called him "the dumb ox." Thomas wanted to become a Dominican priest. These were very poor priests who had a simple lifestyle of prayer that Thomas really liked. His family, though, was against this idea. In fact, they locked Thomas in the family castle for a whole year hoping he would change his mind, but he didn't! When they finally released him, he did indeed become a Dominican priest. Thomas loved God with all his heart and wrote five important books on Christianity.

Opening Prayer

God our strength,
help us to be more like the saints
who show us that
what matters most in life
is not what we own,
or who we know,
or the job we do;
what really matters
is how much faith, love and trust
we have in God
and how well we show these
in all that we do.

Help us to learn that
there are many ways to follow Christ.
Amen.

Final Instructions and Greetings
(adapted from 1 Thessalonians 5:12-24)

A reading from the first letter of Paul to the Thessalonians

It is right friends to be respectful to those who work with you, who guide you and who instruct you in the Christian life. Treat them with the greatest respect and love because of the work they do. Do not fight amongst yourselves; be at peace.

It is also important to try to not be lazy, to encourage the shy person, to help the weak and to be patient with everyone. Make sure that you don't pay back a wrong with a wrong, but always try to do good for one another and to all people.

Finally, always be cheerful, pray everyday and be thankful in all circumstances. This is what God wants you to do in following Jesus Christ. Keep what is good and avoid every kind of evil.

May the God who gives us peace, make you holy in every way and keep your whole being—spirit, soul and body—free from every fault.

The word of the Lord.
Thanks be to God.

Petitions

Lord God,
we ask that you help us
to be more like St. Thomas Aquinas.
The response to each petition is:
Lord, help us to be more like St. Thomas Aquinas.

That we will pray to God everyday …
we pray to the Lord.
Lord, help us to be more like St. Thomas Aquinas.

That we will study hard in school and learn all that we can … we pray to the Lord.
Lord, help us to be more like St. Thomas Aquinas.

That we might learn to follow God's word with faith and love … we pray to the Lord.
Lord, help us to be more like St. Thomas Aquinas.

That we may always treat others as we would like to be treated … we pray to the Lord.
Lord, help us to be more like St. Thomas Aquinas.

That we always try to do our best and that we ask for God to forgive us for our sins … we pray to the Lord.
Lord, help us to be more like St. Thomas Aquinas.

That we always try to do our best and that we take responsibility for any mistakes we may make … we pray to the Lord.
Lord, help us to be more like St. Thomas Aquinas.

That we will always ask questions and keep searching for answers, for it is in the search that we grow … we pray to the Lord.
Lord, help us to be more like St. Thomas Aquinas.

That we may appreciate and protect our world's wonders, both in nature and in the animal kingdom … we pray to the Lord.
Lord, help us to be more like St. Thomas Aquinas.

Closing Prayer

God our loving Father,
help us to be more like St. Thomas.
Teach us to put our trust in you,
as he did.
Teach us to love others:
in the classroom,
in the schoolyard,
in our homes
and in our neighbourhood.

May St. Thomas and all the saints
guide our steps in goodness,
befriend us in loneliness
and strengthen us in danger.
We ask this in the name of
your Son, Jesus Christ,
our way, our truth and our life,
who lives
and reigns with you,
one God forever and ever.
+ Amen.

February

1. Black History Month: Celebrate, Learn and Love

*The Lord says to his people,
"I have always loved you."*
(Malachi 1:2)

Introduction

+ Every year in February, we are invited to celebrate and learn about the many experiences, achievements and contributions of black individuals. Throughout history, the black community has played a vital role in making our country the culturally diverse, compassionate and prosperous nation we know today.

Many, many years ago, however, this was not the case. In this troubled time, blacks were enslaved. They had little or no freedom. It is hard for us to imagine how this was so. But imagine being whipped if someone thought you didn't work hard enough. Imagine working from sunrise to sunset everyday and not being paid anything for your work. Imagine being bought or sold away from your family like cattle.

Later on, even when blacks were not slaves, life was far from easy. Imagine not being allowed to sit where you liked on a bus. Imagine not being allowed to vote or go to schools with clean rooms, solid furniture, new books, and paper, pencils and erasers for everyone. We have come a long way since those difficult times.

It is important for us to remember these times so that we don't repeat mistakes of the past. Instead, we learn to celebrate the present and look ever forwards to a brighter future.

During Black History Month, let us celebrate the contributions of black individuals and learn to accept all people of the world with love and respect.

Let us listen to the word of God. Today, it explains that God has chosen all of us to be his special people.

You are the People of God
(adapted from Colossians 3:12-14)

A reading from the letter of Paul to the Colossians

Brothers and sisters,
God loves you and has chosen you all as his own special people.
Put up with each other and forgive anyone who does wrong,
just as Christ has forgiven you.
Love is more important than anything else. It is what ties everything completely together.

The word of the Lord.
Thanks be to God.

Litany: Let Us Celebrate

There are too many people to name them all individually. Let the names listed below represent all those in similar fields who have given so much to us today. Let us celebrate their accomplishments and give thanks to God for their lives.
All: We are called to celebrate. We are called to learn. We are called to love.

Let us celebrate freedom fighters who looked for equality for blacks, such as Martin Luther King Jr., Harriet Tubman, Rosa Parks and Josiah Henson.
All: We are called to celebrate. We are called to learn. We are called to love.

Let us celebrate the fastest and the best, such as sprinter Donovan Bailey and boxer Muhammad Ali.
All: We are called to celebrate. We are called to learn. We are called to love.

Let us celebrate writers, such as Maya Angelou and Rosemary Brown.
All: We are called to celebrate. We are called to learn. We are called to love.

Let us celebrate entertainers, such as Oprah Winfrey, Michael Jackson and Bill Cosby.
All: We are called to celebrate. We are called to learn. We are called to love.

Let us celebrate those in authority, such as Nelson Mandela, Desmond Tutu and Barack Obama.
All: We are called to celebrate. We are called to learn. We are called to love.

Let us honour the contributions of all black people, past and present, during Black History Month.
All: We are called to celebrate.
We are called to learn.
We are called to love.
Amen.

Closing Prayer

Loving God,
May we always celebrate
the contributions of all around us.
May we learn to appreciate
the differences between us.
May we offer true respect and love to all.
We ask this through your Son Jesus,
our guide in all celebrations,
learning and love.
+ Amen.

2. God's Gift of Wisdom

I will speak words of wisdom.
(Psalm 49:3)

Opening Prayer

+ God of all knowledge,
we thank you for the gift of wisdom.
We know that as Catholics,
using wisdom means that
we listen to our conscience
to be our guide
in everything we do.
Wisdom means that we try to use
all the gifts we have been given
for the good of all.
May we appreciate the gift of wisdom
as we come to know you better.
Amen.

The Bible speaks to us about wisdom.

Jesus and the Festival
(adapted from John 7:10-18)

A reading from the holy Gospel according
to John
Glory to you, Lord.

It was the time for the Festival of Booths
and Jesus' disciples had gone on ahead to
celebrate. There were a lot of people there
and so when Jesus came much later on,
many did not notice that he had arrived.
During this time, some of the people there
began to speak about Jesus.

*Students mill about as if they are at a festival. Some
stop in the centre and have the following conversation.*

Some were saying: "Where is Jesus?
He should be here by now!"
Two students go off looking for Jesus.

Others were saying, "That Jesus is a good
man!"

But there were many who were afraid that
the Jewish authorities would overhear them,
so said, "Oh no, he's not good at all. I hear
that he plays tricks on people."

A little while later, in the middle of the
festival, Jesus went to the temple and began
to teach the people there. Many people
gathered around him to hear his words.
*(Have some students form a small crowd around
Jesus, with some sitting at his feet and listening to his
words.)*

Jesus said, "Let me tell you about the
Kingdom of God."

The Jewish authorities standing near the
back of the crowd were astonished and said,
"How does this man have such wisdom
when he has never been formally taught?"

Jesus heard them and said to them, "My
wisdom does not come from me but rather
from God, who sent me. Anyone who
promises to follow God's word will understand. They will know that this wisdom
comes from God. Those who speak on their
own will only be trying to get glory for
themselves. But those who speak from God
will grow in truth and wisdom."

The Gospel of the Lord.
Praise to you, Lord Jesus Christ.

Litany: Wisdom

Wisdom can't be taught.
We gain wisdom through experience.
**All: May we use God's gift of wisdom all
our lives.**

Wisdom can't be passed on
from someone who is wise
to someone who is foolish.
We have to gain wisdom on our own.
**All: May we use God's gift of wisdom all
our lives.**

You don't get tested on wisdom
in school.
Wisdom isn't something that you
pass or fail,
because you can't get marked for it.
**All: May we use God's gift of wisdom all
our lives.**

Jesus tells us that wisdom
comes from God.
God's wisdom calls us to love others
as ourselves, to share our gifts
and to always follow our conscience in
everything we do and say.
**All: May we use God's gift of wisdom all
our lives.**

The wisdom God gives to each of us
can make us happy.
It allows us to feel the gentle
guiding hand of God in our lives.
Wisdom allows the light of God
to shine from each of us
so that others may learn
to trust in him, too.
Wisdom brings us closer to God.
**All: May we use God's gift of wisdom all
our lives.**
+ Amen.

3. Love and Friendship

Friends always show their love.
(Proverbs 17:17)

Opening Prayer

+ Loving Jesus,
we thank you for the gift of friendship.
Our friends
play with us, encourage us,
share with us, keep our secrets,
rejoice with us when we succeed,
stay with us when we are sad
and bless us always with their love.
May we be ever thankful for our friends.
Amen.

Let us listen to the words that Jesus spoke about loving others.

The Greatest Commandment
(Mark 12:28-29)

A reading from the holy Gospel according to Mark
Glory to you, Lord.

A teacher of the Law came to Jesus with a question. "Which commandment is the most important of all?" Jesus replied, "The most important one is this: "Listen Israel! The Lord our God is the only Lord. Love the Lord your God with all your heart, with all your soul, with all your mind and with all your strength ". The second most important commandment is this: "Love your neighbour as you love yourself. There is no other commandment more important than these two."

The Gospel of the Lord.
Praise to you, Lord Jesus Christ.

Friendship Prayer

Right side: We are blessed by our friends. We are sure of their love.
Left side: We can be ourselves knowing we won't be made fun of.

Right side: We are blessed by our friends. In them we can trust.
Left side: They know all our secrets and keep them because they must.

Right side: We are blessed by our friends. We can give and give and give.
Left side: We gain more in return and happier lives we live.

Right side: We are blessed by our friends. With them we laugh, cry and play.
Left side: With our friends close beside us, we work together every day.

Right side: We are blessed by our friends. We pray with them to our Lord.
Left side: We know that as God's children we are adored.
Both: Thank you, God, for friends. Amen.

Closing Prayer

God of friendship,
help us to always treat others
with love and respect,
for we know that Jesus calls us
to love others
as we love ourselves.
May he walk with us every day
and guide us in our relationships.
May we always appreciate
the wonderful gift of our friends.
We ask this through your Son Jesus.
+ Amen.

4. Daughters and Sons of Faith

"Let the children come to me."
(Mark 10:14)

Introduction

+ Most of the Bible stories that we read are about faithful men and women who followed the word of God. Let us listen to three Bible stories about children who were faithful to the word of God.

The Story of Samuel
(adapted from 1 Samuel 1–3)

Hannah was married to a man named Elkanah. They had no children. Hannah promised God that if he granted her a son, she would take him to the temple and dedicate his life to God. God answered her prayers and she had a son whom she named Samuel. In order to keep her promise, when Samuel was a little boy, she took him to the priest named Eli. The boy Samuel served the Lord under Eli. Every year Hannah would return to visit and pray at the temple. She would bring her son a new robe that she had made for him.

One night, young Samuel heard a voice call his name. He got out of bed and went to Eli and said, "You called me and I am here." Eli told him to go back to bed because he hadn't called him. A second time, Samuel heard a voice call him by name. Again he went to Eli, who told him to go back to bed. When Samuel returned a third time, Eli realized that it was the Lord calling. Eli told Samuel that when he heard the voice again, he should answer, "Speak, Lord, your servant is listening."

God called a fourth time. This time Samuel answered, "Speak, Lord, your servant is listening."

God told Samuel about things that would come to pass. He also spoke of Eli's two wicked sons, who would die on the same day. All these things came true.

Samuel continued to serve the Lord and grew up to be a well-liked prophet and ruler who always followed the word of God.

Naaman's Little Servant Girl
(adapted from 2 Kings 5:1-27)

There once was a commander of the Syrian army named Naaman. During one of the raids against Israel, a little Israelite girl was captured. He and his wife took her in as a servant girl. Naaman had developed a terrible skin disease, which caused him a lot of pain. Even though the little servant girl had been taken from her family, she still believed in the power of God and wished that her master would be healed.

One day, the little servant girl said to Naaman's wife that she had heard of a prophet, Elisha, who she believed would be able to cure the Commander. She suggested that Naaman go and see him. Naaman decided to listen to her and went to Elisha as she had suggested. Elisha healed him! Naaman tried to pay Elisha 3,000 silver pieces for his services, but Elisha refused, asking only that he worship the one true God.

Through the faith of a little girl, a great commander was healed.

Josiah
(adapted from (2 Kings 22–23)

Josiah became king when he was only 8 years old. He was a faithful boy and wished that all in his kingdom would worship the one true God.

At the time Josiah became king, many of the people worshipped pagan gods instead of the one true God. He decided to give money to pay all the carpenters and the masons to rebuild and repair all the temples to God.

A book containing the word of God was found. After it was read to him, Josiah had it read aloud to all the people and so restored the true faith to them. After he had done this, he took down all the temples to the pagan gods and all now worshipped the one true God.

Even though he was young, Josiah made a big difference in the lives of his people because of his faithfulness.

Litany: Daughters and Sons of Faith

Let us pray for children who follow their faith and listen to the word of God, for they will ever be blessed by God.
All: Let us be daughters and sons of faith.

Let us make a positive difference in the faith life of those around us.
All: Let us be daughters and sons of faith.

Let us remember that nobody is too small, too young or too unimportant in the eyes of God. Everyone counts.
All: Let us be daughters and sons of faith.

Let us follow God's Word and live as Jesus shows us.
All: Let us be daughters and sons of faith.

Let us share our faith with all we meet: our friends in the schoolyard, our fellow students in the classroom, the teachers and administrators who help us to learn, our priests and our families and neighbours.
All: Let us be daughters and sons of faith.
Let us follow the word of God.
Amen.

Closing Reflection

There are many other stories in the Bible about children. Others include David, the young boy who defeated the giant Goliath because he knew that the power of God was on his side (1 Samuel 17:1-54) and Joseph, the young dreamer who never gave up his faith in God, becoming governor of Egypt and forgiving his brothers who had sold him into slavery (Genesis 37–50).

Jesus said that grown-ups need to be like children in order to enter the Kingdom of Heaven (Matthew 18:3).

Children like you are the future. Our faith rests within your hands. We need to remember that what all these stories have in common is very important. All of them deal with children who listened to the word of God and applied it to their lives. Let us remember the children we have heard about today. Let us read their stories and learn from their faithfulness. Let us pass on their steadfast faith to future generations. May we also learn to be daughters and sons of faith.
+ Amen.

5. A Time for Ashes: Ash Wednesday

*I am going to take her
into the desert again;
there I will win her back
with words of love.*

(Hosea 2:14)

Opening Prayer

+ God of justice and love,
prepare our hearts
for the Lenten season.
Lead us to the quiet and simple places
where we can hear your voice.
We are sorry for the times
when we have forgotten you,
when we have hurt others and ourselves.
Lead us back to holiness.
We pray in the name of Jesus.
Amen.

Jesus in the Desert

(Mark 1:12-15)

A reading from the holy Gospel according
to Mark
Glory to you, Lord.

At once the Spirit made him go into the
desert, where he stayed forty days, being
tempted by Satan. Wild animals were there
also, but angels came and helped him. After
John had been put in prison, Jesus went to
Galilee and preached the Good News from
God. "The right time has come," he said,
"and the Kingdom of God is near! Turn
away from your sins and believe the Good
News!"

The Gospel of the Lord.
Praise to you, Lord Jesus Christ.

Responsorial Prayer

On Ash Wednesday,
we mark the beginning of Lent
by marking our foreheads
with a cross of ashes.
All: May these ashes be a sign of our sorrow.
Lent is a time of simplicity.
All: Let us simplify our lives.
Lent is a time of opening our hearts.
All: Let us open our hearts to Jesus.
Lent is a time to give up things that stop us
from being close to Jesus.
All: Let us draw closer to Jesus.
Lent is a time of prayer.
All: Let us pray alone and together.

Our Father

Knowing that Jesus is with us
on our Lenten journey,
we pray the prayer that Jesus taught us.
Our Father …

Closing Prayer

Loving God,
may we accept your invitation
to walk with you,
to listen to you,
to pray with you,
to be with you.
Let these forty days of Lent
be a sacred time of healing
and forgiveness.
May every step we take
make us draw closer to you.
In your holy name we pray.
+ Amen.

March

1. Lent I: Desert

Sin is crouching at your door.
It wants to rule you,
but you must overcome it.

(Genesis 4:7)

Introduction

+ During Lent, we are asked to fast in order to renew our hearts. This means giving up a treat or doing something special to become a more loving person. It can often be a very difficult thing to do for the 40 days of Lent and we can be tempted to stop. Jesus himself was tempted by Satan in the desert for 40 days. But if we manage to sacrifice that treat or make an effort to do that special something, we open our hearts and souls to God.

Let us listen to the story of Jesus being tempted in the desert.

The Temptation of Jesus in the Desert
(adapted from Matthew 4:1-11)

A reading from the holy Gospel according to Matthew
Glory to you, Lord.

The Spirit led Jesus into the desert to be tempted by the Devil. After spending forty days and nights without food, Jesus was hungry.

Then the Devil came to him and said, "If you are God's Son, then order these stones to turn into bread."

But Jesus answered, "The scripture says, 'Human beings cannot live on bread alone, but need every word that God speaks.'"

Then the Devil took Jesus to Jerusalem, the Holy City, and set him on the highest point of the Temple, and said to him, "If you are God's Son, throw yourself down, for the scripture says, 'God will give orders to his angels about you; they will hold you up with their hands, so that not even your feet will be hurt on the stones.'"

Jesus answered, "But the scriptures also say, 'Do not put the Lord your God to the test.'"

Then the Devil took Jesus to a very high mountain and showed him all the kingdoms of the world in all their greatness, "All this I will give you," the Devil said, "if you kneel down and worship me."

Then Jesus answered, "Go away, Satan! The scripture says, 'Worship the Lord your God and serve only him!'"

Then the Devil left Jesus; and angels came and helped him.

The Gospel of the Lord.
Praise to you, Lord Jesus Christ.

Ritual

Write down the treat that you intend to give up during Lent or the action that you intend to do during Lent to become more caring. Remember that this is a secret promise between you and God. There is no need to share what you have written with anyone else.

When you are finished writing, fold your piece of paper and write your name on the outside in brightly coloured letters. Nobody is going to read what is inside. During the Litany that follows, you are to come up quietly and place your folded piece of paper into this black box. Black symbolizes the darkness of the tomb. This box will be shut and put away just as you will try to "put away" your temptations for all of Lent. At Easter, the box will be opened and you will retrieve your own paper. (These can be displayed with the brightly coloured names showing to reflect the joy of the Easter Season.)

Litany: Lead Us Not into Temptation

It is often very hard to resist temptation. Sometimes we think we can get away with doing something we shouldn't, without anyone seeing us. We pray:
All: **Lead us not into temptation.**

We may be watching TV and our favourite show comes on, yet we have a lot of homework to do. We pray:
All: **Lead us not into temptation.**

We may be trying to cut down on junk food and eat a more healthy diet but when we get our allowance we want to buy chocolate bars and candy. We pray:
All: **Lead us not into temptation.**

We know that we're supposed to take turns using the computer in class, but we really want to play a game on it and nobody has noticed that we have finished our assigned task. We pray:
All: **Lead us not into temptation.**

We have a messy floor beneath our desk. Nobody else is in the room so we think about sweeping the mess under our neighbour's desk. We pray:
All: **Lead us not into temptation.**

God sees and knows all. God knows how difficult it is for us to sometimes resist temptation, but God always calls us to do our best to do what is right.
All: **Lead us not into temptation, but deliver us from evil. Amen.**

Closing Prayer

When we pray the Our Father,
we ask God's help to
"lead us not into temptation,
but deliver us from evil."
As we close with this prayer,
let us remember the promises
we have made to God
for this Lenten season.
Let us pray for God's help
to stay the course
and not give into temptation.
Our Father …
+ Amen.

2. Lent II: Prayer

I pray to you, O Lord;
you hear my voice.

(Psalm 5:2-3)

Introduction

+ During Lent, we are asked to make a special effort to pray every day. When we pray, we speak to God: we praise, worship and thank God for our many blessings. We also ask for forgiveness for any wrongs we have done. We know that as children of God, we are especially loved. During this season, we are encouraged to pray often. Praying helps us to grow in our faith.

The Bible speaks to us about prayer.

Ask, Seek, Knock
(adapted from Matthew 7:7-11)

A reading from the holy Gospel according to Matthew
Glory to you, Lord.

Jesus said,

"Ask and you shall receive. Seek and you will find. Knock and the door will be opened to you. For everyone who asks will receive, and anyone who seeks will find and the door will be opened to those who knock.

"Would any of you give your child a stone when he asks for bread? Or would you give your child a snake when she asks for a fish?

"You know how to give good things to your children. How much more then, will your Father in heaven give good things to those who ask him."

The Gospel of the Lord.
Praise to you, Lord Jesus Christ.

When Do We Pray?

We can pray with our community
when we attend Mass.
This is special because
we share the bond
of belonging to the family of God.
All: Let us pray with our community when we attend Mass.

We can pray as a school.
This is special because
our school shares the bond
of learning together.
All: Let us pray with our school.

We can pray with our classmates.
This is special because
our classmates share a bond
of friendship.
All: Let us pray with our classmates.

We can pray with our families.
This is special because
our families share a special bond
of love.
All: Let us pray with our families.

We can pray when we are alone.
This is special because
we can share everything
with the One who loves us
no matter what.
All: Let us pray when we are alone.

No matter when we pray,
we know that God is listening.
This is special because
we are the children of God.
All: Let us pray to God the Father who loves us.

Ritual

In order to speak to God, sometimes we need silence. Take a moment and clear your mind. Think of what you would like to say to God today. Speak to God silently in your heart.

Let us pray in thanksgiving. Let us thank God for all the good things he has given us …

Let us pray in worship. Let us offer our silent prayers of praise to God …

Let us pray for forgiveness. Let us offer up our sins for God with sorrowful hearts …

Let us pray for others in our community. Let us offer prayers for any in the community who are suffering in any way …

Jesus taught us a special prayer. Let us close our prayer service by praying together in the way that he taught us: **Our Father** … **+ Amen.**

3. Lent III: Almsgiving

When you give to the poor,
it is like lending to the Lord,
and the Lord will pay you back.

(Proverbs 19:17)

Introduction

+ During Lent, it is important to remember those who are less fortunate than we are. This includes the poor in spirit and the poor in wealth, the ill and the lonely. What we give can be different for each person. We can give our prayers, our time or even a smile. During this season, we are encouraged to give of ourselves to those in need. This helps us to grow in our faith.

The Final Judgement
(adapted from Matthew 25:34-40)

A reading from the holy Gospel according to Matthew
Glory to you, Lord.

Jesus (*offstage*): **The King will say to the people on his right, "Come, you that are blessed by my Father! Come and possess the kingdom which has been prepared for you ever since the creation of the world. I was hungry and you fed me, thirsty and you gave me a drink; I was a stranger and you received me in your homes; naked and you clothed me …**

When did I do these things? I never gave you food. I never gave you anything to drink. I never gave you clothing. I never welcomed you when you were alone.

Jesus (*offstage:*) **Whenever you showed compassion by doing these things for any other person, you did it for me.**

The Gospel of the Lord.
Praise to you, Lord Jesus Christ.

Litany: Let Us Give

All: Let us give to those who hunger.
We can give food to our local food bank.
All: Let us give to those who are poor.
We can share what we have.
All: Let us give to those who are lonely.
We can visit them.
All: Let us give to those who have few friends.
We can share a smile and play with them.
All: Let us give to those who are ill.
We can offer our prayers to God
for their healing.
Amen.

Closing Reflection

Jesus taught us how to give.
He gave us the greatest gift of all.
He gave up his life that we might live.
He asks only that we love God first,
with all our hearts,
and then love our neighbours.
We can show our love for God
in our prayers
and in the way we live our lives,
following God's word.
We can show our love
for our neighbours
by freely sharing our gifts.
Let us give to others.
+ Amen.

4. Forgiveness

*"Forgive anything you may have
against anyone,
so that your Father in heaven
will forgive the wrongs
you have done."*

(Mark 11:25)

Introduction

+ Today, we are going to listen to a story of a father who had two sons. It is a story of forgiveness. We ask God's help to always have open hearts to forgive others, especially when it is difficult.

The Prodigal Son
(Luke 15:11-32)

A reading from the holy Gospel according to Luke
Glory to you, Lord.

There once was a man who had two sons. The younger one said to him, "Father, give me my share of the property now." So the man divided his property between his two sons.

After a few days, the younger son sold his part of the property and left home with the money. He went to a country far away, where he wasted his money in reckless living. He spent everything he had.

Then a severe famine spread over that country, and he was left without a thing. So he went to work for one of the citizens of that country, who sent him out to his farm to take care of the pigs. He wished he could fill himself with the bean pods the pigs ate, but no one gave him anything to eat.

At last he came to his senses and said, "All my father's hired workers have more than they can eat, and here I am about to starve! I will get up and go to my father and say, 'Father, I have sinned against God and against you. I am no longer fit to be called your son; treat me as one of your hired workers.'" So he got up and started back to his father.

He was still a long way from home when his father saw him; his heart was filled with pity, and he ran, threw his arms around his son, and kissed him. "Father," the son said, "I have sinned against God and against you. I am no longer fit to be called your son."

But the father called to his servants. "Hurry!" he said. "Bring the best robe and put it on him. Put a ring on his finger and shoes on his feet. Then go and get the prize calf and kill it, and let us celebrate with a feast! For this son of mine was dead but now he is alive; he was lost, but now he has been found." And so the feasting began.

In the meantime, the older son was out in the field. On his way back, when he came close to the house, he heard the music and dancing. So he called one of the servants and asked him, "What's going on?" "Your brother has come back home," the servant answered, "and your father has killed the prize calf, because he got him back safe and sound."

The older brother was so angry that he would not go into the house; so his father came out and begged him to come in. But he spoke back to his father, "Look, all these years I have worked for you like a slave, and I have never disobeyed your orders. What have you given me? Not even a goat for me to have a feast with my friends! But this son of yours wasted all your property, and when he comes back home, you kill the prize calf for him!"

"My son," the father answered, "you are always here with me, and everything I have is yours. But we have to celebrate and be happy, because your brother was dead, but how he is alive; he was lost, but now he has been found."

The Gospel of the Lord.
Praise to you, Lord Jesus Christ.

Litany: Teach Us to Forgive

Teach us, O Lord, to always forgive others. We know that forgiveness can be hard to give, especially if we are hurting, but we also know that it is the right thing to do. For you always love us and forgive us all our sins. Forgiveness brings us closer to you.

When people call us names,
All: Teach us to forgive them.

When friends don't play with us,
All: Teach us to forgive them.

When someone talks behind our backs,
All: Teach us to forgive them.

When others are not truthful,
All: Teach us to forgive them.

When classmates take our things without asking permission,
All: Teach us to forgive them.

When people are mean to us,
All: Teach us to forgive them.

For all who hurt us,
All: Teach us to forgive.

May we learn to always offer forgiveness. May we learn to always love others. We ask this through your Son, Jesus Christ.
All: Amen.

Reflection: The Forgiveness Equation

Forgiveness is an equation that has two equal partners: the one who opens their heart and forgives, and the one who is sorry and repents. Both partners are equally important and must balance in the forgiveness equation.

Each of us needs to work hard to be the best we can be, no matter which side of the forgiveness equation we are on, in order to maintain peace and harmony in our lives. It isn't an easy task. We need God's help to be successful.

So as we go out into the schoolyard and into our classrooms today, we must ask ourselves which side of the forgiveness equation we are on. Are we truly sorry for something we have done, or do we need to forgive someone who has wronged us? With God's help, we can balance this equation.

Closing Prayer

Let us close this prayer service with the words that Jesus taught us.
Our Father …
+ Amen.

5. We Need to Persevere: The Story of Zacchaeus

*"Whoever holds out to the end
will be saved."*

(Mark 13:13)

Introduction

+ Perseverance means sticking to our goals. During Lent, this means trying to keep our Lenten promises. When we persevere with prayer, forgiveness and acts of goodness, we renew our hearts.

The Bible speaks to us about perseverance.

Jesus and Zacchaeus
(adapted from Luke 19:1-9)

A reading from the holy Gospel according to Luke
Glory to you, Lord.

Jesus was passing through a town named Jericho. In this town, there lived a very rich tax collector named Zacchaeus. Now Zacchaeus was very curious and wanted to see this Jesus he had heard so much about. So he went to stand by the road where Jesus was going to pass.

Zacchaeus was a short man and the crowd was so thick that he couldn't even catch a glimpse of Jesus! He was very disappointed but he didn't give up. Zacchaeus was persistent and so he persevered. He decided to run ahead of the crowd and to climb a sycamore tree so that when Jesus passed him, he would be able to see him from the tree.

When Jesus came by a little later, he looked up into the tree and saw Zacchaeus up there and said to him, "Zacchaeus, come down from that tree! Hurry! I am going to have dinner at your house!"

Zacchaeus was surprised but pleased as well. He quickly climbed down and welcomed Jesus. All the people in the crowd, though, began to grumble among themselves, saying, "How could Jesus go to *his* house?" and "That Zacchaeus is a sinner!"

Zacchaeus, however, was overcome with joy, for having persevered he had been able to see the Lord. He looked at Jesus and promised, "Lord, please listen! I will give half of what I own to the poor, and if I have ever cheated anyone, I will pay them back four times what I owe them!"

Jesus said, "Because this man has persevered, he has been saved. For I came to find and save those that were lost."

The Gospel of the Lord.
Praise to you, Lord Jesus Christ.

Litany: Perseverance

All: God our Creator, we need to persevere.
We will thank you for our lives
and the lives of those around us.
All: God of peace, we need to persevere.
We will pray for the end of all war
for all nations.
All: God of patience, we need to persevere.
We will do our best to keep our Lenten promises.
All: God of love, we need to persevere.
We will love and respect all people of all races.
All: God of life, we need to persevere.

We will thank you for providing us with food, shelter and our families.

All: God of hope, we need to persevere.

We will pray for those who are less fortunate than we are.

All: God of faith, we need to persevere.

We will share our gifts with our neighbours.

All: God of wonder, we need to persevere.

We will look for ordinary miracles every day.

All: God our Saviour, we need to persevere.

We will continue to praise your Son, Jesus Christ.

All: God of all, we need to persevere.

+ Amen.

April

1. Holy Week in Jerusalem

Jesus entered Jerusalem.

(Mark 11:11)

Opening Prayer

+ Dear Jesus,
let us walk with you, step by step,
by your side in that last week in Jerusalem
to your final meal with your friends
and your journey along
the painful road to Calvary.
May we always know
that you are our loving companion.
Amen.

Jesus and Jerusalem

(Mark 10:33-34)

A reading from the holy Gospel according
to Mark
Glory to you, Lord.

Jesus took the twelve disciples aside and
spoke of the things that were going to
happen to him. "Listen," he told them,
"we are going up to Jerusalem where the
Son of Man will be handed over to the
chief priests and the teachers of the Law.
They will condemn him to death and then
hand him over to the Gentiles, who will
make fun of him, spit on him, whip him,
and kill him; but three days later he will
rise to life."

The Gospel of the Lord.
Praise to you, Lord Jesus Christ.

Litany: Jesus in Jerusalem

You entered in Jerusalem in joy and humility.
All: Let us walk in joy and humility.

You taught about justice and peace.
All: Let us walk in justice and peace.
You gathered your friends together at
the Last Supper.
**All: Let us always remember that meal
at Mass.**
You prayed in the garden.
All: Let us walk with you prayerfully.
You were arrested and tortured.
All: Let us always help the hurting.
You were crucified.

(All kneel for a few moments in silence)

Your body was taken down from the cross
and taken again into your mother's arms.
**All: Let us always give comfort to those
who mourn.**
You were placed in the tomb,
where your body stayed
until Easter morning.
All: Let us always walk in the hope of Easter.

Our Father

We pray in unity with all Christians,
Our Father …

Closing Prayer

God of hope,
always guide our footsteps.
Give us prayerful hearts,
always open to your guiding love.
Give us mindful hearts,
always aware of others' needs.
Give us just hearts,
always ready to do your work.
We pray in the name of Jesus:
betrayed, tortured, crucified and risen.
+ Amen.

2. Easter Joy!

*Shout for joy to God
our defender.*

(*Psalm* 81:1)

Opening Prayer

+ On that blessed morning, loving God,
Mary went to the tomb
to find that Jesus had risen!
May our prayers join the prayers
of heaven in joy and love.
Together we say:
All: Love has conquered death.
We say with joy:
All: Love has conquered death.
We say with love:
All: Love has conquered death.

The Resurrection
(Luke 24:1-6a)

A reading from the holy Gospel according
to Luke
Glory to you, Lord.

Very early on Sunday morning the women
went to the tomb, carrying the spices they
had prepared. They found the stone rolled
away from the entrance to the tomb, so
they went in; but they did not find the
body of the Lord Jesus. They stood there
puzzled about this, when suddenly two men
in bright shining clothes stood by them.
Full of fear, the women bowed down to the
ground, as the men said to them, "Why are
you looking among the dead for one who is
alive? He is not here; he has been raised."

The Gospel of the Lord.
Praise to you, Lord Jesus Christ.

Resurrection Prayer

Loving God,
the signs of new life we see outside remind
us of the resurrection.
May warmer days
All: remind us of the warmth of your love.
May spring flowers
All: remind us of your beauty.
May the new green around us
All: remind us of your hope.
May birdsong in the morning
All: remind us of your joy.

Easter Alleluia

With all the angels and saints,
with all of God's good people,
we proclaim our Easter alleluia:
Alleluia, Christ is risen!
All: Alleluia, Christ is risen!
Alleluia, Christ is risen!
Alleluia, Christ is risen!

Closing Prayer

God of Easter hope,
help us to be signs of new life
to one another,
to our families,
to our community.
We make this prayer
in the name of the risen Jesus,
Christ for ever and ever.
+ **Amen.**

3. The Journey: The Road to Emmaus

I will prepare a road
for my people to travel.

(Isaiah 49:11)

Introduction

+ Jesus walks with us every day. When we play in the schoolyard and when we learn in the classroom, when we laugh, when we cry, when we pray and when we sing, Jesus always walks with us. So as we journey through our lives, even though we do not see Jesus, it is wonderful to know that we are not alone.

The disciples also knew that Jesus walked with them every day. Today we will read a story of one time when Jesus was walking on the road with two of his disciples but they didn't recognize him. This happened three days after Jesus had been crucified.

The Bible speaks to us about the journey.

The Road to Emmaus

(adapted from Luke 24:13-35)

A reading from the holy Gospel according to Luke

Glory to you, Lord.

On the first day of the week, two of the disciples were going to a village called Emmaus, which was about eleven kilometres from Jerusalem. As they walked, they were speaking to each other about all the things that had happened. While they were talking to each other, Jesus himself came near and walked with them, but they did not recognize him.

And Jesus said to them, "What are you talking about while you are walking?" They stopped walking for a moment, looking sad. Then one of them, whose name was Cleopas, answered him, "Are you the only person in Jerusalem who does not know the things that have taken place here in the last few days?" Jesus asked them, "What things?"

The first disciple replied, "The things about Jesus of Nazareth. Don't you know? Haven't you heard about him? Jesus was a mighty prophet, mighty in everything he did and said. But our chief priests and leaders handed him over to be condemned to death. Then they crucified him. But we had hoped that he was the one who would save us."

The second disciple then continued, "It's been three days since these things all happened. And do you know that some of the women of our group shocked us this morning? They were visiting the tomb of Jesus very early in the morning and they didn't find his body there! Then they came back and told us that they had seen a vision of angels who said that he was alive. Some of us who heard this then went to the tomb ourselves and found it just as the women had said; but we didn't find Jesus anywhere."

Then Jesus said to them, "Why did that surprise you? Wasn't it written that the Messiah had to suffer all these things before entering into his glory?" Then Jesus explained to the disciples all the things about himself that had been written in the scriptures. The disciples listened to him and were amazed that this stranger had so much information about Jesus, but they still didn't recognize him.

As they came near to Emmaus, Jesus walked on ahead as if he was going to continue on the road on his own, but the two disciples stopped him, saying, "Stay with us. It is almost evening and it's getting late." So he went in to stay with them. When he was at the supper table with them, he took the bread, blessed and broke it, and gave it to them. Suddenly their eyes were opened and they recognized him! And at that very moment, Jesus vanished from their sight!

The two disciples couldn't believe that they had not recognized Jesus before this. They said to one another, "Weren't our hearts just burning when he explained all about himself in the scriptures?"

They got up right away and returned to Jerusalem that same night and found the other disciples and their companions gathered together. The other disciples told the two who had been walking to Emmaus that Jesus had indeed risen and had appeared to Simon, another disciple. Then the two disciples also told what had happened on the road to Emmaus and how they recognized Jesus in the breaking of the bread.

The Gospel of the Lord.
Praise to you, Lord Jesus Christ.

Journey Prayer

God of the journey,
on days when everything
seems to be going our way,
we know that you are there
celebrating with us.
We need to remember
to pray in thanksgiving
for all of our blessings.
All: We thank you for walking with us on our good days.

When things are not going so well,
we need to still remember that
you journey with us,
offering your support and love.
At these times we still offer you praise.
All: We thank you for walking with us on our bad days.

At all times in our lives, during the bad and good and in between, we need to remember to pray often. We thank you for journeying with us.
All: We thank you for walking with us always.

May we continue to offer you our grateful thanks and praise as we journey with you always.
+ Amen.

4. Signs of New Life: Earth Week

God looked at everything he had made,
and he was very pleased.

(*Genesis 1:31*)

Opening Prayer

+ God of creation,
you bless this beautiful world
and ask us to take special care of this, our
home.
Give us the wisdom and courage
to heal the places
where the earth is hurting,
we turn our ears and hearts
to you for guidance this day.
Amen.

God's Majesty

(adapted from Psalm 8:1, 3-9)

A reading from the Book of Psalms

O God, our God!
how majestic is your name
in all the earth!
You have set your glory
above the heavens.
When I consider your heavens,
the work of your hands,
the moon and the stars,
which you have set in place,
You made us a little lower
than the heavenly beings
and crowned us with glory and honour.
you put everything under our feet:
all flocks and herds,
and the beasts of the field,
the birds of the air,
and the fish of the sea,
all that swim the paths of the seas.

O God, our God
how majestic is your name
in all the earth!

The word of the Lord.
Thanks be to God.

Prayer of Creation

God of all goodness,
All: Let us learn from your creation.
The patience and dignity of an oak tree:
All: Let us learn from your creation.
The joy and beauty of the morning song of
the goldfinch:
All: Let us learn from your creation.
The strength and power of water weaving
among solid rocks:
All: Let us learn from your creation.
Let us turn these lessons into gifts for the
earth –
not just good words but also blessings:
blessings of planting trees,
blessings of cleaning up trash,
blessings of reducing energy.

Closing Prayer

Loving God, bless our eyes
so that we can see the beauty of your
creation.
Bless our minds
so that we can find ways
of healing our wounded world.
Bless our hands
so that we can go out
to bring your peace and justice
to this planet.
We make this prayer in the name of Jesus,
healer and teacher.
+ **Amen.**

5. The Wonder of Creation: Let Us Be Reverent

The Lord formed and made the earth —
he made it firm and lasting ...
a place for people to live.

(Isaiah 45:18)

Opening Prayer

+ God of creation,
We thank you for the wonder of creation.
We know that you made everything
we see around us:
the day, the night,
the sky, the sun, the stars,
the oceans, the plants, the fish,
the birds, the animals,
and all the people in the world.
May we always worship you with awe and
reverence.
Amen.

God speaks to us in the Bible about the
wonder of creation.

Creation
(adapted from Genesis 1:1-30)

A reading from the Book of Genesis

In the beginning, God created the heavens
and the earth.

God said, *"Let there be light!"* And there
was light. And God saw that it was good.

God separated the light from the darkness
and called the light "Day" and the dark
"Night."

On the second day, God created a dome in
the middle of the waters. God said, *"Let the
dome be separated from the waters."* And

it was so. And God saw that it was good.
He called the dome "Sky."

On the third day, God said, *"Let the waters
under the sky be gathered into one place
and let the dry land appear."* And it was so.
And God saw that it was good. He called
the dry land "Earth" and the waters "Seas
and Oceans."

On the fourth day, God said, *"Let there
be lights in the sky in the day and in the
night."* And it was so. And God saw that
it was good. He called the light in the day
"Sun" and the lights in the night "Stars."

On the fifth day, God said, *"Let there be
living things and living creatures in the
waters and in the skies."* And it was so.
And God saw that it was good. He called
the living things and creatures in the waters
"Fish," "Seaweed" and "Underwater Plants,"
and the creatures in the skies "Birds."

On the sixth day, God said, *"Let there be
living things and living creatures on the
surface of the earth."* And it was so. And
God saw that it was good. He called the
creatures "Cattle," "Lions," "Squirrels," "Deer"
and all the other animals of the earth, and
called the other living things "Flowers" and
"Trees."

Then God said, *"Let there be human
beings made in my image. Let these
humans rule over all the other animals and
living creatures on earth. Let them use
plants and seedlings for food and to make
shelter and tools. Let them make the land
and seas of earth as their home."* And it
was so. And God saw that it was good.

He breathed life into the humans and
blessed them, making male and female.
He called the humans "Man" and "Woman."

Then God looked at all he had made.
The day and the night, the sky, the land
and the seas, the sun and the stars, the living
creatures in the oceans, the skies and the
earth, and the humans in God's own image.
And God saw that it was very good.

The word of the Lord.
Thanks be to God.

Litany: Reverence

Let us join in faith and walk with reverence
together to the Lord.
We know that the road is long
but we never need to be afraid,
for when we walk the road
with reverence,
we know that Christ is here with us.

We cherish and protect creation.
This beautiful world was a gift to us
from God.
All: Let us be reverent, O God.
We appreciate the gift of creation.

We thank God for all the people in our
lives, who love and support us, keep us safe
and help us to learn.
All: Let us be reverent, O God. We are
thankful for all those who surround us.

We praise God for the gift of his Son, Jesus
our Saviour.
All: Let us be reverent, O God. We praise
you for sending us Jesus.

We honour and respect God's gift of life.
All: Let us be reverent, O God. We thank
you for the blessing of life.
May we walk with reverence to you all the
days of our lives.
+ Amen.

May

1. Mary, Queen of Peace

"You are the most blessed of all women."

(Luke 1:42)

Opening Prayer

+ Loving Jesus,
in this month of Mary,
we turn our hearts
to your Blessed Mother.
May she be an example to us
as she was to you:
an example of love, wisdom and hope.
Help our hearts listen
to the words of the Gospel.
Amen.

Mary's Song of Praise

(Luke 1:46-49)

A reading from the holy Gospel according
to Luke
Glory to you, Lord.

Mary said,
"My heart praises the Lord;
my soul is glad because of God my Saviour.
for he has remembered me,
his lowly servant!
From now on all people will call me happy,
because of the great things the Mighty God
has done for me."

The Gospel of the Lord.
Praise to you, Lord Jesus Christ.

Litany: Mary, the Teacher

Mary, you obeyed the call of God:
All: Teach us to listen.
Mary, you carried the sacred in your words:
All: Teach us to respect life.
Mary, who fled to a far-off land:
All: Teach us to always return to our true home.
Mary, you raised your cherished son:
All: Teach us also in grace and truth.
Mary, you called Jesus to help others at Cana:
All: Teach us to reach out to others.
Mary, you stood at the foot of the cross:
All: Teach us hope, even in darkness.

Hail Mary

Let us join in the special prayer to the
mother of Jesus …
Hail Mary …

Closing Prayer

Loving God,
Mary answered your call
to bring divine love into the world.
May we follow Mary's path
and bring your love
to the people we meet
on our journeys.
In the name of Jesus,
whose mother is the Queen of Peace.
+ Amen.

2. God Bless Our Mothers

*Respect your father
and your mother.*

(Exodus 20:12)

Opening Prayer

+ Loving God,
Soon it will be Mother's Day.
We ask you to continue to bless
our mothers.
May they always be teachers
of love and wisdom.
May they always be models
of kindness and courage.
May they always be touched
by your grace and truth.
We make this prayer
in the name of Jesus.
Amen.

Hymn to Love
(1 Corinthians 13:4-8a)

A reading from the letter of Paul to
the Corinthians

Love is patient and kind; it is not jealous or
conceited or proud; love is not ill-mannered
or selfish or irritable; love does not keep a
record of wrongs; love is not happy with
evil, but is happy with the truth. Love never
gives up; and its faith, hope, and patience
never fail. Love is eternal.

The word of the Lord.
Thanks be to God.

Litany: Our Mothers

For their care and concerns,
All: We are grateful.
For their wisdom and knowledge,
All: We are grateful.
For their compassion and forgiveness,
All: We are grateful
For their smiles and hugs,
All: We are grateful.
For their love and protection,
All: We are grateful.
For their warmth and strength,
All: We are grateful.
For their work and play,
All: We are grateful.
For giving us life,
All: We are grateful.

Hail Mary

We pray to Mary, the mother of Jesus,
her special prayer:
Hail Mary …

Closing Prayer

Loving God,
bless and care for our mothers always.
May they always be beloved
and cherished.
Help us to be grateful and helpful,
not just on Mother's Day but every day.
We make this prayer
in the name of Jesus,
who loved his own mother very much.
+ **Amen.**

3. Celebrating the Eucharist

"Take and eat this bread," Jesus said;
"this is my body."
(Matthew 26:26)

Introduction

+ Jesus is present when we break bread, reminding us of his body being broken for us. Wine is a drink of celebration. When wine is poured, it reminds us of Jesus pouring out his blood for us. Let us celebrate being invited to God's banquet, the Eucharist.

I Am the Bread of Life
(adapted from John 6:32-33, 35)

A reading from the holy Gospel according to John
Glory to you, Lord.

Jesus said to the people,

"It is my Father who gives you the real bread from heaven, for the bread that God gives, is He who comes down from heaven and gives life to the world.

"I am the bread of life. Whoever comes to me will never be hungry, and whoever believes in me will never be thirsty."

The Gospel of the Lord.
Praise to you, Lord Jesus Christ.

Litany: You Are the Bread of Life

Jesus, you are the Bread of Life.
You have promised that we will never be hungry for your love.
All: You are the Bread of Life.

You offer us eternal life with you in heaven.
All: You are the Bread of Life.

You protect us in times of trouble and support us in times of happiness.
All: You are the Bread of Life.

You are in all that we are and all that we seek to be.
All: Praise to You, Lord Jesus.
You are the Bread of Life.

Jesus, we thank you for the sacrifice you made for us.
We thank you for your gift of love and life.
All: You are the Bread of Life.

We offer you our praise and love.
All: You are the Bread of Life.

We seek to live under your loving protection and support.
All: You are the Bread of Life.

We try to live our lives following your word.
All: Praise to You, Lord Jesus.
You are the Bread of Life.

We will never grow hungry
when we share the Bread of Life.

Closing Prayer

God of life,
may we be ever thankful
for the gift of Jesus,
who gave his life for us.
May we always remember his sacrifice
in the breaking of the bread.
We ask this through your Son,
Jesus Christ our Lord,
who is the Bread of Life.
+ Amen.

4. Confirmation: Spirit, Flow Through Us

God has poured out his love
into our hearts
by means of the Holy Spirit ....
(Romans 5:5)

Opening Prayer

+ Creator God, giver of life,
Jesus Christ, healer and teacher,
Holy Spirit, love overflowing,
bless your children
as we celebrate their Confirmation.
May they always trust in you
and be open to your love.
Open the eyes of our hearts
to hear the story of your Spirit
flowing among us.
We make this prayer
through the power of the Holy Spirit.
Amen.

Pentecost
(Acts 2:1-4)

A reading from the Acts of the Apostles

When the day of Pentecost came, all the
believers were gathered together in one
place. Suddenly there was a noise from
the sky which sounded like a strong wind
blowing, and it filled the whole house where
they were sitting. Then they saw what
looked like tongues of fire which spread out
and touched each person there. They were
all filled with the Holy Spirit and began to
talk in other languages, as the Spirit enabled
them to speak.

The word of the Lord.
Thanks be to God.

Litany: Pentecost

At Pentecost,
we celebrate the Confirmation
of the presence of the Holy Spirit
on the first Christians.
We pray for wisdom
to be aware of God's loving presence:
All: Holy Spirit, flow through us.
We pray for understanding to know
the truth:
All: Holy Spirit, flow through us.
We pray for right judgment to choose
goodness:
All: Holy Spirit, flow through us.
We pray for the courage to act on our
beliefs:
All: Holy Spirit, flow through us.
We pray for knowledge to see God's ways:
All: Holy Spirit, flow through us.
We pray for reverence for all of creation:
All: Holy Spirit, flow through us.
We pray for awe of God's vast creation:
All: Holy Spirit, flow through us.

Closing Prayer

Holy Spirit,
Bless those who are being confirmed.
May you lead them to lives
overflowing with goodness and grace.
May their eyes shine with your grace;
may they speak of faith, hope and love;
may their deeds be as true as their words;
may they always be open
to your inspiration and leadership.
We make this prayer in the joy and hope of
the Pentecost Spirit.
+ Amen.

5. We Are Called to Be Responsible

Everyone has to carry his own load.
(Galatians 6:5)

Introduction

+ We are called to be responsible. When we are responsible, we care for all members of God's family, at home, at school and in our community.
All: **We are called to be responsible.**
God cares for us all.
We are reliable so that others can depend on us.
All: **We are called to be responsible.**
We can always depend on God.
We keep the promises we make to all those in our communities.
All: **We are called to be responsible.**
God keep all of the promises he makes to us.

The Bible speaks to us about responsibility.

The Widow's Offering
(adapted from Mark 12:41-44)

A reading from the holy Gospel according to Mark
Glory to you, Lord.

Jesus sat near the Temple treasury and watched the people as they dropped in their money. Many rich men dropped in a lot of money. Then he saw a poor widow who dropped in two little copper coins. He called his disciples together and said to them, "I tell you that this poor widow has put more into the offering box than all the others combined. For the others offered their gifts from what they had to spare of their riches, but she, poor as she is, put in all she had. She gave all she had to live on."

The Gospel of the Lord.
Praise to you, Lord Jesus Christ.

What does this story tell us about responsibility?

The story is saying that even if you have only a little to give, it is welcome. Don't measure your gifts by the size of others' gifts. Do what is expected of you and be responsible for your actions because you are a caring family member.

Jesus the Good Shepherd
(adapted from John 10:11-16)

A reading from the holy Gospel according to John
Glory to you, Lord.

Jesus said to his disciples,
"Listen to this story:
I am the good shepherd and I look after my sheep. Their care is my responsibility. When the hired man, who does not own the sheep, sees a wolf coming, he leaves the sheep and runs away. Then the wolf takes one sheep and the rest scatter. The hired man runs away because he does not care about the sheep. I am the good shepherd. I am responsible for my sheep. As God the Father knows me, so I know my sheep and they know me. And I am willing to die for them. There are other sheep that belong to me that are not in this sheep pen. I will look for them and find them and bring them safely in to the pen."

The Gospel of the Lord.
Praise to you, Lord Jesus Christ.

What does this story tell us about responsibility?

Jesus is telling us that we are his family and that no matter what, we can depend on him to be there for us. Jesus is teaching us to be responsible for those around us. Do not be like the hired man in the story who runs away when there is work to do. Be responsible!

Abraham and Sarah
(adapted from Romans 4:18-21)

Abraham knew that God could make things come to life with just a word. So even when Abraham was 100 years old and his wife Sarah was 90, Abraham believed and trusted in God's word. God said that Sarah and Abraham would have a son. God told him that he, Abraham, would be the father of many nations and that his children's children would be more plentiful than the stars in the sky. Abraham's faith did not leave him. He trusted in God's power and gave God praise. He was absolutely sure that God would be able to do what he had promised.

Sarah and Abraham did indeed have a son. They named him Isaac.

The word of the Lord.
Thanks be to God.

What does this reading tell us about responsibility?

God keeps all the promises that he makes to us. God is telling us that when we make a promise, we should keep it. Others need to know that they can depend on us. Keeping our promises is the responsible thing to do.

Reflection: Responsibility

Responsibility means we can be relied on.
Each of us is called to do our part.
Sharing our faith and love means that our
Promises are given from the heart.
On our life's journey, we
Need to always remember that we can
Show others we can help to carry the load
If they need a hand.
Because we know that
It is our responsibility to
Love others and to treat them
In a kind way, so with smiles we greet them.
Take care and be responsible to the end.
You'll find God will always be your friend.
+ Amen.

June

1. We Are God's Works of Art

God's temple is holy,
and you yourselves are his temple.
(*1 Corinthians* 3:17)

Opening Prayer

+ God of the universe,
you lead us along paths of beauty;
you teach us to love;
you grace us with imagination and wonder.
We thank you
and we bless your holy name.
Amen.

God Knows Us

(Psalm 139:1-5)

A reading from the Book of Psalms

Lord, you have examined me and
you know me.
You know everything I do;
from far away you understand all my
thoughts.
You see me, whether I am working
or resting;
you know all my actions.
Even before I speak,
you already know what I will say.
You are all around me on every side;
You protect me with your power.

The word of the Lord.
Thanks be to God.

God's Artistry

God, you have created us to love;
to bring your peace
and justice to the world.
All: We are your works of art.
Each cell, each fibre of our bodies
is a marvel.
All: We are your works of art.
Our thoughts, dreams and loves
reach beyond ourselves to you.
All: We are your works of art.
Loving God,
Open our eyes to our own beauty.
We can create, calculate and compose.
All: We are your works of art.
We explore, question and reflect.
All: We are your works of art.
We laugh, we mourn and we comfort.
All: We are your works of art.

Closing Prayer

Creator God,
you have wondrously made us;
you bless us with so many gifts;
May we also be your gifts
to each other and to the world.
We make this prayer
in the name of Jesus.
+ **Amen.**

2. Lead Us to the Truth: Honesty

All my words are sincere,
and I am speaking the truth.

(Job 33:3)

Opening Prayer

+ God of truth,
Guide us always on the road
to what is right and true.
We know that is isn't always easy
to be honest. It can be hard work.
With your help and guidance,
we can learn to be sincere
and trustworthy in all we say,
write and do.
Lead us to the truth, O God.
All: Amen.

The Bible speaks to us about honesty.

The Faithful and the Unfaithful Servant
(adapted from Luke 12:41-47)

A reading from the holy Gospel according to Luke
Glory to you, Lord.

Jesus says:
"Who is the honest and faithful servant?
He is the one that the master puts in charge
to run the household. The master trusts him
to give the other servants their jobs for the
day and their share of the food at the proper
time. This honest servant will be happy
when his master comes home and finds
him doing exactly what was asked of him.
In fact, the master will put the honest and
faithful servant in charge of all his property.

"Who is the dishonest and unfaithful
servant? He is the one who would say to
himself that his master is taking a long time
to come back, and then begin to mistreat
the other servants. He would even eat and
drink all the food himself! So when the
master comes back when the servant does
not expect him and sees that he has been
dishonest and unfaithful, the master will be
very angry and will punish this servant for
being unfaithful.

"The servant who knows what his master
wants him to do but does not do it is
unfaithful and will be punished severely.
The servant who knows what his master
wants and does it will be rewarded because
he is faithful."

The Gospel of the Lord.
Praise to you, Lord Jesus Christ.

Litany: Lead Us to the Truth

In our schools, in our homes and in the
community, God calls us to be honest,
faithful and true. Lead us to the truth,
O God.
All: Lead us to the truth, O God.

We are honest when we speak the truth to
our teachers, to our families, to our friends
and to everyone we meet.
All: Lead us to the truth, O God.

When we do not lie, we are honest.
All: Lead us to the truth, O God.

We are honest when we are respectful of others and when we listen attentively when others are speaking.
All: Lead us to the truth, O God.

When we do not hurt other people's feelings, we are honest.
All: Lead us to the truth, O God.

We are honest when we do what is right and true.
All: Lead us to the truth, O God.

When we are faithful and follow our word, we are honest.
All: Lead us to the truth, O God.

We are honest when others know that they can trust us.
All: Lead us to the truth, O God.

When we keep our promises, we are honest.
All: Lead us to the truth, O God.

God of honesty,
we ask that you lead us always
in the path of truth,
for we know that when we are honest,
you are pleased with us.
We ask this through Christ our Lord.
+ Amen.

3. Rainbows: God's Covenant

*"I am putting my bow in the clouds.
It will be the sign of my covenant
with the world."*

(Genesis 9:13)

Introduction

+ Whenever we see a rainbow in the sky we enjoy the pretty colours that we can see because they reflect the light of the sun. But rainbows also represent a promise made by God to all people. The bible tells us about this promise.

The Story of Noah

(adapted from Genesis 6:9-22; 7:4,13-17, 20, 23-24; 8:6)

A reading from the Book of Genesis

This is the story of Noah.

Noah had three sons, Shem, Ham and Japheth and was the only good man of his time. He lived in fellowship with God but everyone else was evil in God's sight and violence had spread everywhere. God looked at the world and saw that it was evil for the people were all living evil lives.

God said to Noah, "I have decided to put an end to all people. I will destroy them completely because the world is full of their violent deeds. Build a boat for yourself out of good timber; make rooms in it and cover it with tar inside and out. Make it 450 feet long, 75 feet wide and 45 feet high. Build it with three decks and put a door in the side. I am going to send a flood on the earth to destroy every living being.

"Everything on the earth will die but I will make a covenant with you. You are to go onto the boat with your wife and your sons and their wives. You will take onto the boat, a male and female of every kind of animal and of every kind of bird, in order to keep them alive. You will need to take along all kinds of food for you and them."

Noah did everything that God had commanded.

The Lord then said to Noah, "Seven days from now I am going to send rain that will fall for forty days and nights." Seven days later, the flood came.

So Noah and his wife went into the boat with their three sons Shem, Ham and Japheth and their wives. And with them went every kind of animal, domestic and wild, large and small and every kind of bird. A male and female of each kind of living being went into the boat with Noah as God had commanded. Then the Lord shut the door behind Noah.

The flood continued for 40 days and the water became deep enough for the boat to float. It became so deep that it covered the highest mountains and it went on rising until it was about 25 feet above the tops of the mountains!

The Lord destroyed everything on earth. The only ones left were Noah and those who were with him on the boat.

After 40 days Noah opened a window and sent out a raven. It did not come back but kept flying around. Meanwhile, Noah sent out a dove to see if the water had come down. The first time it could not find another place to land because the water had not gone down so it came back. Seven days later, Noah sent out the dove again. This time it returned with a fresh olive branch in its beak so that Noah knew that the water had gone down.

God said to Noah, "Go out of the boat with your wife and your sons and their wives. Take all the birds and animals out with you that they might reproduce and spread all over the earth."

So Noah went out of the boat with his wife and sons and their wives. All the animals and birds went out of the boat in groups of their own kind.

God then said to Noah, "Never again will I destroy human beings as I have done this time. It will be a sign of my covenant to the world. Whenever I cover the sky with clouds and the rainbow appears, I will remember my promise to you and to all the animals. That is the sign of the promise which I am making to all living things."

The word of the Lord.
Thanks be to God.

Prayer: The Rainbow is a Promise

All: May we shine like a rainbow, showing off our beautiful colours.
We are asked to share all our gifts
and not hide them inside.
In sharing what we can offer,
we make the world a brighter
and more colourful place.

All: May we reach to the sky like a rainbow, arching towards heaven.
We are called to reach for heaven
by living as Jesus taught us.
When we do this,
we draw closer to God.

All: May we shine after the rain like a rainbow bright.
We shine when we treat others
with compassion and respect.
This can be as simple as sharing a smile
to cheer up a friend,
saying something nice
to a person who is sad
or visiting someone who is lonely.

All: May we remember our promises, just as God gave the rainbow as a sign of his promise.
We need to remember
to always keep our word
when we make promises to others.
This way they know
they can depend on us.
God keeps all the promises
he makes to us.
May we learn to be as faithful.
Amen.

Closing Prayer

God of promise,
help us to recognize
the beauty of a rainbow,
the beauty of your promise to us.
Help us to be people
who follow your Word, as Noah did.
We ask this through your Son, Jesus.
+ Amen.

4. Graduation: Moving On

Since you are God's dear children,
you must try to be like him.
Your life must be controlled by love ....
                                    (Ephesians 5:1-2)

Opening Prayer

+ Loving God,
We celebrate the gift
of our graduates today.
As they leave our school,
we honour them
and ask you to bless them.
May your wisdom always guide them along
paths of goodness.
We make this prayer
in the name of Jesus.
Amen.

Rejoice!

(Philippians 4:4-9)

A reading from the letter of Paul to
the Philippians

May you always be joyful in your union
with the Lord. I say it again: rejoice! Show
a gentle attitude toward everyone. The
Lord is coming soon. Don't worry about
anything, but in all your prayers ask God
for what you need, always asking him with
a thankful heart. And God's peace, which is
far beyond human understanding, will keep
your hearts and minds safe in union with
Christ Jesus. In conclusion, my brothers
and sisters, fill your minds with those things
that are good and that deserve praise: things
that are true, noble, right, pure, lovely, and
honourable. Put into practice what you
learnt and received from me, both from my
words and from my actions. And the God
who gives us peace will be with you.

The word of the Lord.
Thanks be to God.

Litany: Graduation

God of all goodness,
we give thanks for the
many gifts and talents
that these graduates
have brought to our school:

For their understanding and compassion,
All: We are grateful.
For their leadership and creativity,
All: We are grateful.
For their joy and kindness,
All: We are grateful.
For their curiosity and imagination,
All: We are grateful.
For these gifts and many others,
All: We are grateful.
For they have been a blessing
to our school.

Closing Prayer

God of all goodness,
Bless these graduates
as they go forward
on their journeys.
Guide them through
challenges and changes.
May they always be a blessing
to their families, their friends
and their communities.
We ask this grace through Jesus Christ,
who lives and reigns for ever and ever.
+ Amen.

5. Words for Your Journeys

*May the Lord bless you
and take care of you.*

(Numbers 6:24)

Opening Prayer

+ Loving Jesus,
we belong to you.
Make our hearts quiet and peaceful
so that we can hear your word
and know who we need to help
and where we need to go.
Amen.

Jesus Commissions the Disciples

(Matthew 28:18-20)

A reading from the holy Gospel according
to Matthew
Glory to you, Lord.

Jesus drew near and said to them, "I have
been given all authority in heaven and on
earth. Go, then, to all peoples everywhere
and make them my disciples: baptize them
in the name of the Father, the Son, and the
Holy Spirit, and teach them to obey everything I have commanded you. And I will be
with you always, to the end of the age."

The Gospel of the Lord.
Praise to you, Lord Jesus Christ.

Discipleship: A Shared Reading

Leader: Jesus sent out his disciples
to tell all people the Good News.
Today, Jesus asks us to do the same – to go
out and tell everyone
the Good News of God's love.

**All: How can I do this?
I am so young!**

Leader: Listen to Jeremiah,
who said the same thing:
"O Lord God! Truly I do not know how to
speak, for I am just a boy."
(Jeremiah 1:1)

Reader 1: God replied, saying,
"Do not be afraid of them,
for I am with you ... " (Jeremiah 1:8)

Reader 2: How do I spread this message,
this Good News?
**All: There will be a time for words
of love and forgiveness.
But first, you need to be a model
of love and forgiveness.**

Reader 3: Do I teach through my kind deeds
and courageous actions?

Reader 4: And standing up for the hurting
and unpopular. Can I do this?

Leader: You have been blessed
by a sense of what is right
and what is wrong.
You have been taught
ways of goodness and truth.
You have a family and friends to help.
You have been taught how to pray.
**All: With God's help,
we will have words for our journeys.**

Closing Blessing

May God bless you
as you go forward as disciples,
to be God's word
and to be God's love to all you meet.
We make this prayer
in the name of Jesus.
+ **Amen.**

Appendix: Preparations and Rituals

This appendix gives suggestions for prayer focal points and rituals you may wish to include in your prayer services. If you use the prayer service during a different liturgical season than the one suggested in the book, then change the coloured cloths to that of the liturgical season or occasion. For all prayer services, explain to all participants beforehand how the prayer, particularly the rituals, will unfold, in order to preserve the sacred atmosphere.

Before the prayer service:

❖ provide copies of the prayer service

❖ set up the liturgical focal point
  Consider including:

  o liturgical cloth

  o candles (votive, pillar or tea lights)

  o crucifix

  o Bible

  o picture or symbol of the school's patron

  o rosary

❖ select the readers

❖ arrange the seating

❖ explain any ritual actions that might take place

September

1. The Journey Begins

To the prayer centre, add symbols of learning, such as books, chalk, a globe, a ball, a paintbrush, a computer keyboard. Use a green cloth for Ordinary Time. As a ritual after the Gospel reading, the teacher may bless each student using words such as these: "May you be blessed now, through this school year and always, in the name of the Father, and of the Son, and of the Holy Spirit." Students respond, "Amen."

2. We Follow Jesus

Use a green cloth for Ordinary Time. For the prayer centre, consider including a fishing net, a student agenda or school year calendar, and educational supplies. If the prayer service is being conducted as a class and you wish to incorporate a ritual, consider holding different parts of the prayer service in different parts of the school. In this way the prayer service is a procession.

3. Sunflowers

You may wish to decorate your prayer focal point with pictures or models of sunflowers made by the students. Scatter some sunflower seeds on your prayer centre. It you wish to place a tablecloth on your prayer centre, it should be green for Ordinary Time.

4. God Gives Us Courage

Students can act out the scripture reading (David and Goliath). They may wish to mime the actions while the narrators read aloud what is happening. This is best done as a classroom prayer service, but can be adapted for the whole school.

5. Jesus Is Our Teacher

Students can act out this prayer service in a classroom setting. This service can also be used as an assembly to be shared with others. In preparing for this Prayer Service, students can read the many biblical stories before presenting to deepen their understanding of the contents.

October

1. God Is in You

Place a green tablecloth on the prayer focal point. Students may choose to use props or dress up in simple costumes to illustrate the different activities mentioned in the litany.

2. We Give Thanks

A green cloth should be the first layer on the prayer centre; however, a smaller gold or orange cloth may be laid on top. Symbols of Thanksgiving – such as a cornucopia, wheat or harvest fruits and vegetables – can be displayed. Consider creating a cross from autumn leaves. Ahead of time, students may write things they are most thankful for on an appropriately coloured maple leaf. During the prayer service, these leaves may be placed in the shape of a cross on the prayer focal point, individually or collectively.

3. Compassion

Place a green tablecloth and a lit green pillar candle on the focal point for prayer. The scripture reading can be acted out. For the Compassion prayer, students can each hold up a letter in the word COMPASSION. You will need 10 students.

4. In the Eyes of God

Students might like to prepare pictures of what they imagine God's eyes might look like and display these as decorations or hold them up during the prayer service.

5. Halloween: Deliver Us from Evil

Use a green cloth for Ordinary Time.

November

1. We Pray with the Saints: All Saints Day

Use a white cloth for your prayer centre. Display pictures of saints, particularly the patron saint of the school. Some schools have a patron saint for each classroom. Consider creating a procession (if in a classroom setting) in which the Litany of the Saints is extended to include all the saints in the school and is proclaimed outside each door. If the service takes place in an assembly, pictures of the saints may be projected during the litany.

2. A Time for Peace

On the green tablecloth, place symbols of peace, including a dove, origami cranes or pictures of famous peacemakers, such as Blessed Mother Teresa of Calcutta, Gandhi, Martin Luther King Jr., St. Francis and, of course, Jesus Christ.

The sign of peace can be simply a nod of the head or turning to each other with a kind word or a handshake.

3. We Remember

On a green cloth, pin or lay poppies in the shape of a cross. You may also include a copy of a Remembrance Day book, such as In Flanders Fields. At the beginning of the two minutes of silence, consider playing "The Last Post"; end the two minutes with "O Canada." Students should stand through this part of the prayer service. This service can be held in conjunction with a guest speaker, such as a veteran.

4. The Golden Rule

Place a green tablecloth on the prayer centre. Ask several students to act out the story while Readers 1, 2, 3, and 4 tell the story. They may dress in costume if they wish. You may want to display the Golden Rule poster published by the Scarboro Foreign Missions in the space as well.

5. We Seek Justice

Create a focal point for prayer using a green tablecloth. You may want to include portraits of figures who represent justice (e.g., Jesus Christ, St. Vincent de Paul, Jean Vanier, Pope John Paul II) and picture books that illustrate justice.

December

1. Advent I: Find Hope

On the prayer table, place a purple tablecloth and an Advent wreath. Assign one student to light the first candle.

2. Advent II: Find Faith

On the prayer table, place a purple tablecloth and an Advent wreath. Assign one student to light the first two candles.

3. Advent III: Find Joy

On the prayer table, place a purple tablecloth and an Advent wreath. Assign one student to light the first three candles.

4. Advent IV: Find Love

On the prayer table, place a purple tablecloth and an Advent wreath. Assign one student to light all four candles.

5. Bless Our Gifts: An Advent Charity Drive

On the prayer table, place a purple tablecloth and an Advent wreath. Before the service begins, light the appropriate number of candles. Around the prayer centre place some of the food, clothing or toys that were collected during the charity drive.

January

1. A New Hope, A New Year

On the prayer centre, place a white cloth (before the Baptism of the Lord) or green cloth (after the Baptism of the Lord). (White is used during the Christmas season.) You may also include New Year's decorations.

2. Unity: We Are One Body

On the prayer centre, place a white cloth (before the Baptism of the Lord) or green cloth (after the Baptism of the Lord). Consider arranging the seating in a circle as a symbol of unity.

Actions for How We See Unity in our School

When heavy loads are carried alone, they can be difficult to lift. (One student tries to carry a heavy box alone.)

When we are united and help each other together to grow, we are much stronger people because unity means that we work together. (Another student comes along and helps to carry the box. Together they do it easily.)

When we are alone, we can often be easily broken. (One student breaks a single twig.)

But like these twigs bound together, it is more difficult to break our spirits. (One student holds many twigs bound together and shows that they cannot be broken.)

3. The Kindness of God's People

On the prayer centre, place a white cloth (before the Baptism of the Lord) or green cloth (after the Baptism of the Lord). Place either one large heart with students' names on it or individual hearts with students' names on them. Consider inviting students to share a sign of peace.

4. Prayers of Comfort at a Time of Loss

This prayer service can be used anytime during the school year after students have experienced a death in the family. Use a cloth with liturgically appropriate colours. Consider inviting students to share a sign of peace. Instruct the reader of the scripture to wait about 20 seconds before reading the next line.

5. St. Thomas Aquinas: Patron Saint of Catholic Schools

Place symbols of learning on a white cloth if the prayer service is held on January 28, the feast of St. Thomas Aquinas. If you have any icons or images of St. Thomas Aquinas, these would be appropriate, too.

February

1. Black History Month: Celebrate, Learn and Love

Display photographs of various famous and not as well known black individuals around the prayer focal point.

2. God's Gift of Wisdom

Place a green tablecloth on the prayer focal point if the prayer service is held before Ash Wednesday and purple if it is held after Ash Wednesday. Students may wish to act out the reading. Suggestions for the inclusion of many students are written throughout the reading.

3. Love and Friendship

If this is being done with a small group of students, choose an area where there is enough room to sit or stand in a large circle to signify an endless circle of love and friendship. In the centre of the circle, place a prayer table with a liturgically appropriate colour.

4. Daughters and Sons of Faith

Use a liturgically appropriate cloth for tabling: green for Ordinary Time or purple for Lent.

5. A Time for Ashes: Ash Wednesday

Note: This is not intended to be a prayer service for the distribution of ashes.

On a purple cloth place ashes, sand, and/or pictures of desert. If you wish to add a ritual, place a bowl with students names in it. Students are to pick a name from the bowl and asked to pray for them during Lent.

March

1. Lent I: Desert

In the centre of the prayer focus place a purple candle to signify God's presence in our desert. Place a glass bowl filled with sand near one side of a bare table. Around the bowl place some small rocks of different sizes and colours. If being done in a classroom, also place a black box on the prayer focus and give every participant a piece of paper to write down the treat that they intend to give up or the action that they intend to do to improve themselves during Lent. They put their name on the outside in brightly coloured letters. Then the students are to fold the papers. Let them know that nobody else will read these. At the end of the service have students place these papers in a black box. Close the box and 'put away' their temptations. The box is not to be opened until after Easter. At this time, the papers can be displayed on a bulletin board with the brightly coloured names facing outward to signfy the great joy of the Easter season and to celebrate the return of the treat students gave up for Lent.

2. Lent II: Prayer

Place a purple candle on the prayer centre to signify God's presence. Drape a purple cloth over the prayer centre. Consider using Lenten symbols such as rocks, sand, and ashes.

During the ritual, allow students to pray to God quietly for a minute after each statement.

3. Lent III: Almsgiving

Place a purple candle on the prayer centre to signify God's presence in our service of others. Consider using Lenten symbols such as rocks, sand and ashes.

4. Forgiveness

Students may wish to act out the scripture reading. You may want to display a copy of Rembrandt's painting entitled The Prodigal Son. Consider using Lenten symbols such as rocks, sand and ashes.

5. We Need to Persevere: The Story of Zacchaeus

Since this season is Lent, the cloth on the table should be purple. You may also wish to decorate with Lenten symbols (e.g. ashes, a sign reading "King of the Jews," a bag of coins, a basin and pitcher). The students may wish to act out the scripture reading.

April

1. Holy Week in Jerusalem

Tell students that at one point in the service they will be asked to kneel if they are able. This action is done instead of using words, since there are no proper words to respond to the crucifixion. On the prayer centre, place a purple cloth, palms, a bowl of water, bread, a chalice, a cross and nails.

2. Easter Joy!

On a white cloth, place Easter symbols such as a lily, a butterfly, and/or a picture of a sunrise. Invite students to exchange a sign of peace.

3. The Journey: The Road to Emmaus

Since this prayer service is held during the Easter season, the cloth and decorations should be gold or white. Decorate with Easter symbols (e.g., lilies to signify new life and/or an empty cross to signify Jesus' triumph over death). Students may wish to act out the scripture reading.

4. The Wonder of Creation: Let Us Be Reverent

In the days before the service, students can make pictures or dioramas depicting what God made on the different days of creation, including light, darkness, sky, oceans, fish, plants, land, animals, birds and humans. These would be displayed at the appropriate times during the reading.

5. Signs of New Life: Earth Week

On a white cloth, place strips of green cloth and natural objects such as plants, rocks, water, soil, a globe, or pictures of nature.

May

1. Mary, Queen of Peace

On a blue cloth (to represent Mary) place items such as a rosary and a statue or picture of Mary.

2. God Bless Our Mothers

On a white cloth (for the Easter season), place a picture or statue of Mary along with some flowers. If students have made cards or other Mother's Day gifts, these can be added to the prayer centre.

3. Celebrating the Eucharist

Place a green tablecloth on the prayer focal point.

4. Confirmation: Spirit, Flow Through Us

On a red cloth, place symbols of Pentecost, including seven pictures of tongues of fire with the names of the gifts of the Holy Spirit, along with oil and water.

5. We Are Called to Be Responsible

Create a focal point for prayer using a lit candle, a green tablecloth and a Bible. Select readers. For the Reflection: Responsibility, choose 14 students: each can hold up a letter in the word RESPONSIBILITY.

June

1. We Are God's Works of Art

On a green cloth, place an easel with a painting, a piece of sculpture, a musical instrument and a mirror. On the mirror, write the words "You are God's works of art".

2. Lead Us to the Truth: Honesty

Place a green tablecloth on the prayer focal point.

3. Rainbows: God's Covenant

Students can act out the story of Noah and the ark and for decoration can draw pictures of the animals lined up two by two. Other colourful decorations can include rainbows.

4. Graduation: Moving On

On a green cloth, place a scroll tied with a ribbon, books and other symbols of learning (pens, rulers, protractor, musical instruments). As a ritual, each graduating student can be called by name to stand after the scripture reading. During the Graduation litany, the other students and the staff extend their right hands toward the graduates in a gesture of blessing.

5. Words for Your Journeys

On a green cloth, place a road map, compass, sandals and an arrow. Invite students to exchange a sign of peace. Ensure that you have assigned four readers the shared reading and any other parts you wish to delegate.

FSC
Recycled
Supporting responsible use
of forest resources
www.fsc.org Cert no. SGS-COC-003153
© 1996 Forest Stewardship Council

MARQUIS
Marquis Book Printing Inc.

Québec, Canada
2010

Printed on Silva Enviro 100% post-consumer EcoLogo certified paper,
processed chlorine free and manufactured using biogas energy.